Crash Course Literature:

A Study Guide of Worksheets for Literature

By Roger Morante

Library of Congress Cataloging-in-Publication Date is available.

ISBN-13: 978-1-7322125-4-1

Writer: Roger Morante
Cover Design: Artwork purchased from 99Designs.com
Cover Artist: Ryanurz
Copy Editor: Erica Brown
Back Cover Photo: Liesl Morante
Publisher Logo: Isabella Morante

To contact the publisher, send an email to the address below:
holden713@gmail.com

Additional copies may be purchased on www.amazon.com or by contacting the author.

Printed in the United States of America

First printing July 2019

Table of Contents

Name_____
Period_____
Date_____

How and Why We Read: Crash Course English Literature #1

1. Do YOU believe that it is important to read? Why or why not? Defend your answer.

_____
_____
_____
_____

2. Analyze the differences between **stories** that are **written down** and stories that are part of an **oral tradition**. Which do YOU prefer and why? Defend your answer.

_____
_____
_____
_____
_____
_____
_____
_____

3. Why do YOU think **grammar** was invented?

_____
_____
_____
_____
_____

4. Briefly analyze how **barriers** can emerge inside of **communication** between two or more people. *Defend YOUR answer using specific example(s) from YOUR life.*

_____
_____
_____
_____

5. Identify and report on what **good writing** with **good language** means to YOU. *Defend your answer with examples.*

_____
_____
_____
_____
_____
_____

How do I cite somebody else's novel or work? *Tips and Tricks*

TIP 1) **Tips and Tricks**
Please cite your examples if your **quote** is someone else's.
Follow the format of inserting **quotation marks** "   " from someone else like "this," said
*Romeo in Act 1 Scene 5 of <u>Romeo and Juliet</u> by William Shakespeare, and like "this,"
exclaimed Ursula in Chapter 14 of <u>100 Years of Solitude</u> (146) by Gabriel Garcia
Marquez.*
Practice citing here or use any extra sentence lines located on the back of this book

_____

_____

TIP 2) **Tips and Tricks**
The number "146" in **parenthesis** at the end of <u>100 Years of Solitude</u> (146) in Tip 1)
refers to the page number where Ursula had an epiphany and says, "It's as if the world
were repeating itself." (Garcia Marquez 145) ****
Practice citing here or use any extra sentence lines located on the back of this book

_____

_____

TIP 3) **Tips and Tricks**
Notice how, once it has been established what book and author YOU are citing YOUR
words from, YOU may then **shorthand** the rest of your **quotes** by referring only to **the
last name of the author** followed by the **page number** of where YOU found the words
YOU are choosing to analyze. **If it spans multiple pages, then write (Garcia Marquez
145-146)
Practice citing here or use any extra sentence lines located on the back of this book

_____

_____

TIP 4) ***Tips and Tricks***
If you have that specific book of <u>Romeo and Juliet</u>, other **derivations** without quotes may
include: **According to Shakespeare** during **Act 1, Scene 5**, Capulet reprimands Tybalt
for trying to start a fight with Romeo at the Capulet feast.
Practice citing here or use any extra sentence lines located on the back of this book

_____

_____

TIP 5) ***Tips and Tricks***
If you are citing a poem say from **Emily Dickinson**'s unnamed poem, cite it by styling
the first line as in, "I heard a Fly buzz-when I died-" as such in order to name the poem.
Practice citing here or use any extra sentence lines located on the back of this book

_____

_____

Of Pentameter & Bear Baiting – Romeo and Juliet Part 1: Crash Course English Literature #2

1) Investigate how William Shakespeare (1582-1616) didn't actually write the story of
   Romeo and Juliet (1597) but changed the **narrative complexity** of it and thus got credit
   for the story.

   _____

   _____

   _____

   _____

2) Explain how **William Shakespeare** offers a more compassionate view of Romeo and
   Juliet than the poem "The Tragicall Historye of Romeus and Iuliet" (1562) by **Arthur
   Brooke** (?-1563), and the popular tale of **Romeo** and **Juliet** inside of The Palace of
   Pleasure (1566) by **William Painter** (1540-1594).

   _____

   _____

   _____

   _____

   _____

3) Point out the **attributes** of **William Shakespeare's** story of Romeo and Juliet that were
   influenced by **Petrarch** (1304-1374).

   _____

   _____

   _____

   _____

4) Analyze how the setting of the story of Romeo and Juliet by **William Shakespeare** in
   Verona, Italy makes the story of love much safer than in **London, England**.

   _____

   _____

   _____

   _____

5) Explain how Romeo and Juliet by **William Shakespeare** was very much a **political** story
   related to what was going on in **England** in the late **16th century**.

   _____

   _____

   _____

   _____

   _____

6) Evaluate the effectiveness that **narrative complexity** plays in relation to the **structure** of the **tragedy** inside of the play <u>Romeo and Juliet</u> by **William Shakespeare.** *Be sure to point out how it advanced the **structure** of **tragedy** as found inside of the works of* **Aristotle** *(384-322 BCE).*

_____
_____
_____
_____
_____
_____
_____
_____
_____
_____

7) Connect the reasons why **peace** and **harmony** return to the streets of **Verona**, **Italy** after the tragic deaths of **Romeo** and **Juliet**.

_____
_____
_____
_____
_____
_____
_____
_____

8) Analyze the function that the poetic structure of **iambic pentameter** plays in <u>Romeo and Juliet</u> by **William Shakespeare**.

_____
_____
_____
_____
_____
_____
_____
_____
_____

9) Evaluate how **Elizabethan playhouses** of the late 16th century **England** were much different than the playhouses today.

_____
_____
_____
_____
_____
_____
_____
_____
_____

Love or Lust – Romeo and Juliet Part 2: Crash Course English Literature #3

1) Explain how **Juliet** expresses her **feelings** and **true love passion** in <u>Romeo and Juliet</u> (1597) by William Shakespeare (1582-1616).

_____
_____
_____
_____

2) Analyze the reasons why **Juliet** rejects **Paris** as a suitor even though **Capulet**, her father, wants her to marry him. *After analyzing the scene in favor of **Romeo**, now develop a* *counterargument that includes a reason or two why YOU think **Paris** would be a better* *match for her than **Romeo**.*

_____
_____
_____
_____
_____
_____

3) Evaluate how the first few acts of <u>Romeo and Juliet</u> could be seen as a **comedy** rather than a **tragedy**.

_____
_____
_____
_____
_____
_____

4) Develop a **logical argument** that shows how **Romeo** and **Juliet** could really be in **love** even though they just met each other. *Defend your argument using **quotes** from the novel* <u>Romeo and Juliet</u>.

_____
_____
_____
_____
_____
_____

5) Connect how the play <u>Romeo and Juliet</u> by William Shakespeare is a **tragedy** about **time** and **youth**.

_____
_____
_____
_____

6) How do the **characters** in <u>Romeo and Juliet</u> deal with making choices while having only limited information? *Cite an **example** or two from the **play** to defend your answer.*

_____

_____

_____

_____

_____

7) Point out and explain what actually kills **Romeo** and **Juliet**, and what they could have done to avoid this tragic **fate**.

_____

_____

_____

_____

_____

_____

8) In your own words, explain how playwright and critic **Harley Granville Barker** (1877-1946) viewed the **tragedy** of <u>Romeo and Juliet</u> by William Shakespeare by analyzing his quote, "Romeo and Juliet is a tragedy of youth as youth sees it."

_____

_____

_____

_____

_____

9) Formulate the ways **Romeo** and **Juliet** try to get everything that they want even in **opposition** to the wants of the **universe** they inhabit.

_____

_____

_____

_____

_____

_____

10) Critique how the ensuing **havoc** caused by **bad luck** experienced by the **star-crossed** lovers leads to the demise of **Romeo** and **Juliet**.

_____

_____

_____

_____

_____

_____

Like Pale Gold -The Great Gatsby Part 1: Crash Course English Literature #4

1) Briefly explain how the **American Dream** plays out in <u>The Great Gatsby</u> (1924) by F. Scott Fitzgerald (1896-1940).

_____

_____

_____

2) Analyze how the U.S. **Civil War** (1861-1865) provided Midwestern transplant **Nick Carraway,** the narrator of <u>The Great Gatsby</u>, with a good amount of money.

_____

_____

_____

3) Apply concepts to understand how **objectification** caused **characters** such as **Jay Gatsby** from <u>The Great Gatsby</u> and **Romeo** from <u>Romeo and Juliet</u> (1597) to die tragically.

_____

_____

_____

4) Assess the **irony** behind the **racist rant** of **Tom Buchannan** at the awkward party in **Chapter 1** of <u>The Great Gatsby</u>.

_____

_____

_____

_____

5) Support the argument that shows how **Daisy** is NOT a good person by assessing the connection between her part in the 1920s **societal system** of **West Egg**, New York City and that between the poor and the rich during the **Civil War** (1861-1865).

_____

_____

_____

6) Formulate a thesis which shows how the novel of <u>The Great Gatsby</u> serves as a harbinger for the upcoming **Great Depression** (1929-1939) in the United States. *(*hint- Assess what is going on in the 1920s along with the spending habits of many Americans.)*

_____

_____

_____

7) Compare and contrast the difference between the parties thrown by the **characters** of **Tom Buchannan** and those thrown by **Jay Gatsby**.

_____

_____

_____

_____

8) Critique the **drunk driving scene** that epitomizes the **American Dream** (according to author F. Scott Fitzgerald) and takes place during **Prohibition** (1920-1933) in the neighborhood of **West Egg**.

_____

_____

_____

_____

9) Analyze the reason why **Jay Gatsby** throws parties even though he doesn't drink. _Include why **Daisy Buchanan** is part of the reason he throws parties in the first place._

_____

_____

_____

_____

_____

10) Draw conclusions as to what the color the **green light** at the end of Daisy Buchanan's dock symbolizes.

_____

_____

_____

_____

_____

11) Connect what the colors of **gold** and **yellow** symbolize in the novel The Great Gatsby.

_____

_____

_____

_____

12) Analyze how **guilt** and **innocence** is difficult to distinguish in the last chapter of The Great Gatsby.

_____

_____

_____

_____

Was Gatsby Great? The Great Gatsby Part 2: Crash Course English Literature #5

1) Explain how **F. Scott Fitzgerald** (1896-1940) deals with **foreshadowing** in his novel
   The Great Gatsby (1925).

   _____
   _____
   _____

2) Explain why **Fitzgerald** heightens the **language** and **pace** inside of The Great Gatsby.

   _____
   _____
   _____

3) Connect how the **language** of The Great Gatsby elevates **Jay Gatsby's** triumphs and
   tragedies to the level of an **epic story**.

   _____
   _____
   _____

4) Analyze the **irony** surrounding why **bootlegger** Jay Gatsby doesn't get **drunk** at his
   parties and even has a large **swimming pool** that he doesn't swim in.

   _____
   _____
   _____

5) Briefly explain the **similarities** between The Tragedy of Romeo and Juliet (1594) by
   William Shakespeare (1564-1616) and The Great Gatsby by **F. Scott Fitzgerald**.

   _____
   _____
   _____
   _____
   _____

6) Explain what **Jay Gatsby** means when he says in The Great Gatsby that a person, "Can't
   repeat the past? Why of course you can."

   _____
   _____
   _____
   _____

7) Apply concepts to understand why YOU think **presidents of the United States** routinely refer back to **previous presidents** during their presidential **inauguration speeches**.

_____

_____

_____

_____

8) Explain how the **character** of **Jay Gatsby** makes a name for himself in the rich upper-class world even though he is not a person of high birth but rather a person of low birth.

_____

_____

_____

_____

_____

9) Why do YOU think that **Jay Gatsby** decided to take the fall for **Daisy Buchannan** after she hits **Myrtle** with his car?

_____

_____

_____

_____

_____

10) Why do YOU think a **society** could be so **two-faced** that the people of **East Egg** in New York would drink **illegal alcohol** -as the **Era of Prohibition** (1920-1933) was in effect- yet also condemn the **bootlegger** (Jay Gatsby) who provided the alcohol for them to drink?

_____

_____

_____

_____

11) Explain the rationale behind the **18ᵗʰ Amendment to the Constitution** (1919), and then explain the counter logic following **21ˢᵗ Amendment** (1933) repealing of the **18ᵗʰ Amendment**.

_____

_____

_____

_____

12) Briefly explain the **morality** of the **East Egg society** in which **Jay Gatsby** resides.

_____

_____

_____

_____

Language, Voice, and Holden Caulfield: The Catcher in the Rye Part 1: Crash Course English
Literature #6

1) Evaluate the **symbology** inside of <u>Catcher in the Rye</u> (1951) by J.D. Salinger ((1919-2010) that drives narrator **Holden Caulfield**'s decisions to make choices surrounding his **fears** of becoming an **adult**.

_____

_____

_____

_____

_____

_____

_____

_____

_____

_____

_____

2) Why do YOU think that nobody listens to **Holden Caulfield**'s questioning of the **adult world**?

_____

_____

_____

_____

_____

_____

_____

_____

_____

3) Rationalize why **Holden Caulfield** would want to **protect innocence** and be a **catcher in the rye** by analyzing Holden's praise of the **Natural History Museum** where he stated that he liked the museum because, "everything always stayed right where it was."

_____

_____

_____

_____

_____

_____

_____

_____

_____

_____

4) Draw conclusions as to why **Holden Caulfield** would see the **adult world** as **phony** citing evidence from the novel <u>Catcher in the Rye</u> to defend your answer.

_____

_____

_____

_____

_____

_____

_____

_____

_____

_____

5) Analyze the reasons why **Salinger** would choose to **minimize** Holden Caulfield's **voice** by using a **passive writing style** along with a **first-person technique** inside of the <u>Catcher in the Rye</u>.

_____

_____

_____

_____

_____

6) Evaluate how **grammar** and **word choice** contribute to Holden Caulfield's **voice** sounding **authentic** in the novel <u>Catcher in the Rye</u> by J.D. Salinger.

_____

_____

_____

_____

_____

7) Explain how Holden's **narrative voice** and usage of **different tenses** make it easier for the reader to **empathize** with him when he begins to crack and break down.

_____

_____

_____

_____

_____

8) Briefly analyze the **effectiveness** of the word, "**listen,**" at the **end of the novel** <u>Catcher in the Rye</u> by J.D. Salinger.

_____

_____

_____

_____

_____

Holden, JD, and the Red Cap-The Catcher in the Rye Part 2: Crash Course English Literature #7

1) Analyze the ways in which **J.D. Salinger** (1919-2010) lost his innocence during **World War II** (1939-1945).

_____

_____

_____

_____

_____

2) How do you think that the experiences of **J.D. Salinger** during **World War II** (1939-1945) shaped his writing style inside of <u>Catcher in the Rye</u> (1951)?

_____

_____

_____

_____

_____

3) Compare **thematic similarities** between the novels <u>Peter Pan</u> (1904) and <u>Catcher in the Rye</u>.

_____

_____

_____

4) Assess how a **catcher in the rye** saving children from getting too close to the **edge of a cliff** could be seen as **heroic**.

_____

_____

_____

_____

_____

_____

5) Connect the significance of when Holden's sister **Phoebe** puts the **red hunting cap** on the head of **Holden Caulfield** at the start of Chapter 13 of <u>Catcher in the Rye</u>.

_____

_____

_____

_____

_____

_____

_____

6) Explain how **Holden Caulfield** is **empathetic** towards his history teacher **Mr. Spencer**.

_____

_____

_____

_____

_____

7) Draw conclusions as to the reasons why YOU think that **J.D. Salinger** did NOT want to be famous.

_____

_____

_____

_____

_____

_____

8) Why do YOU think that most people are **self-involved** and see themselves as the **central character** in a story instead of expressing **empathy** towards others?

_____

_____

_____

_____

_____

_____

9) Analyze how the **red hunting cap** aids worn by **Holden Caulfield** aids in our understanding to see an **unreliable narrator** as a **heroic character**.

_____

_____

_____

_____

_____

10) Cite evidence as to how the **hunting cap**, the **passive voice**, the **Natural History Museum,** and the **carousel** weighs into **Holden**'s actions in choosing not to grow up. _Defend your answer using examples from the novel **Catcher in the Rye**._

_____

_____

_____

_____

_____

_____

Before I Got My Eye Put Out – The Poetry of Emily Dickinson: Crash Course English Literature #8

1) Point out and explain some examples where **Emily Dickinson** (1830-1886) **contradicts** herself inside of the **light verse** of her poem,"Faith is a Fine Invention," written in 1860 but published after her death in 1891.

   _____
   _____
   _____
   _____
   _____
   _____
   _____

2) Analyze how Emily Dickinson imagines **seeing** as a **power** in her poem, "-I heard a Fly buzz-when I died-," which was written in 1862 but published after her death in 1896.

   _____
   _____
   _____
   _____

3) Analyze how Emily Dickinson plays with the **homonyms**, "I" and "eye" in her poem #327, "Before I got my eye put out-," in order to establish **ownership**.

   _____
   _____
   _____
   _____
   _____

4) Explain how Emily Dickinson's poetry mirrors an **American view in conflict**.

   _____
   _____
   _____
   _____
   _____
   _____
   _____

5) Investigate and report on the **idiosyncrasies** of the life of Emily Dickinson, and report on how that shaped her **character**.

   _____
   _____
   _____
   _____
   _____
   _____
   _____

6) Assess how Emily Dickinson saw the color **white** as representational of **passion** and **intensity**. *Cite examples from her poetry to defend your answer.*

_____

_____

_____

_____

_____

7) Critique Emily Dickinson's use of **dashes** inside of her poem. *Then develop a* **counterargument** *defending why* **dashes** *might be useful in poetry.*

_____

_____

_____

_____

_____

8) Draw conclusions as to why YOU think Emily Dickenson may have been obsessed with **death**. *Cite evidence from Dickinson's poems to defend your answer.*

_____

_____

_____

_____

_____

_____

_____

9) Analyze how in the poem, "I heard a Fly buzz," employs the use of both **trimeter** and **tetrameter iambic lines**. *Include how her use of* **slant rhyme** *creates a discomforting lack of* **closure** *inside the poem.*

_____

_____

_____

_____

_____

_____

10) In your own words, what is **poetry** and what does it mean to YOU?

_____

_____

_____

_____

_____

_____

Tip 6) **Tips and Tricks**Notice that the epic poems of the *Odyssey* and the *Illiad* do not have dates published next to them like <u>Frankenstein</u> (1817) by Mary Shelly nor are they underlined. This is because an exact date is not known and they are epic poems. The epic poem of the *Odyssey* was first written near the end of the 8th century BCE whereas the *Illiad* was written sometime in the 8th century BCE.

Tip 7) **Tips and Tricks**

BC/AD or BCE/ACE?

BCE refers to Before Common Era whereas CE refers to Common Era. In the course of this workbook, BCE is commonly used as a placeholder to aid in understanding of when books were written and to record the passage of time. Standard Western acknowledgement of the passage of time normally has BC which is a confusing English acronym which means Before Christ and AD means Anno Domini or in the year of the Lord with the example 2019 AD symbolizing the year this book was written in Latin. The Latin usage of Anno Domini, as can be seen, only further confuses the issue as both Latin and English are used to describe the passage of time instead of just one common language.

Tip 8) **Tips and Tricks**

What are the origins of AD?

Some secular translations of time prefer the acronym ACE or After Common Era to AD which in my opinion also confuses the issue but at least it is secular and inclusive of all and not just a Judeo-Christian centric view of the universe. This workbook prefers BCE to denote the time period before AD that would otherwise be BC. AD is written ACE but then again, it can be confusing so I choose not to use.

b) For more research on the subject of why time is reported in this BC and AD fashion. I encourage students and scholars to research its mainstream popularity with the 9th century pontiff Holy Roman Emperor Charlemagne (742-814), who loosely based his tracking of time as set up in the Julian calendar established by **Julius Caesar** (100 BCE-44 BCE). Later, the Gregorian calendar introduced by Pope Gregory XIII (1502-1585) in 1582 also played a role in modern AD time tracking. Although, of note, origins of the **Anno Domini Era** (i.e. 1 AD- 2019 AD) trace back to a sixth century monk named **Dionysius Exiguus** (470-544).

Tip 9) **Tips and Tricks**

Notice that the play <u>Hamlet</u> (1599-1602) by William Shakespeare (1564-1616) has multiple dates of publication following it. These dates show when <u>Hamlet</u> was written. It is interesting to note that the first performance of <u>Hamlet</u> occurred in 1609.

_____
_____
_____
_____
_____
_____
_____
_____
_____
_____

A Long and Difficult Journey, or The Odyssey: Crash Course Literature 201 #10

1) Briefly analyze what is known about the life of the Greek poet **Homer** who lived during the 8th century BCE, and was the author of *The Odyssey,* which was composed near the end of the 8th century BCE.

_____
_____
_____

2) Evaluate the subject of the **Trojan War** (1260-1180 BCE) of which the author Homer captured in the aftermath of *The Odyssey* centuries later.

_____
_____
_____
_____

3) Explain why *The Odyssey* is considered to be a **long epic poem**.

_____
_____
_____
_____

4) Provide a brief recap of the major events in *The Illiad* which occurred 10 years before *The Odyssey* and during the **Trojan Wars**.

_____
_____
_____
_____
_____
_____

5) Recap the major event which occurred inside of *The Odyssey*.

_____
_____
_____
_____

6) Evaluate the **heroic characteristics** of **Odysseus** by analyzing a few examples of his **character** inside of *The Odyssey*.

_____
_____

_____

_____

_____

_____

7) Analyze how **overconfidence** proves to be a **fatal flaw** of **Odysseus** during his encounter with the **Cyclops** in _The Odyssey_.

_____

_____

_____

_____

_____

8) Why do YOU think the **Greeks** considered **Odysseus** to be a **hero** regardless of all his negative qualities as a trickster, a liar, a pirate, and as a serial adulterer?

_____

_____

_____

_____

_____

9) Analyze the **double standard** that **Odysseus** has towards **women** inside of _The Odyssey_.

_____

_____

_____

10) Analyze the advice **King Agamemnon** gives to **Odysseus** when they meet in the **underworld**.

_____

_____

_____

_____

_____

11) Explain how **Penelope**, wife of **Odysseus**, tests the faithfulness of her husband.

_____

_____

_____

_____

12) Analyze how **Odysseus** exhibits **Post Traumatic Stress Disorder** (PTSD) after his time fighting in the **Trojan War** inside of _The Illiad_ due to his actions in _The Odyssey_.

_____

_____

_____

_____

Fate, Family, and Oedipus Rex: Crash Course Literature 202 #11

1) Briefly evaluate the reasons why the **Theban clan** of <u>Oedipus Rex</u> (441 BCE) by Sophocles (497-405 BCE) was so **dysfunctional** and tragic.

_____

_____

_____

_____

_____

2) Analyze why the life of **Oedipus** is upended by a **murder investigation** during his reign as **King of Thebes** after solving the **Riddle of the Sphinx** and saving his city from destruction.

_____

_____

_____

_____

_____

_____

_____

3) Draw conclusions as to why **theatre** was equivalent to **civil duty** by the **Greeks**.

_____

_____

_____

_____

4) Analyze the **structure** of **Greek theatre**.

_____

_____

_____

_____

_____

_____

_____

5) Critique the ideas of **Aristotle** (384-322 BCE) and cite evidence as to why many of his ideas are still **controversial** today.

_____

_____

_____

_____

6) Construct a brief **counterargument** as to why people might see **Aristotle** as a good philosopher and powerful **Greek** thinker.

_____
_____
_____

7) Formulate a **concise theory** as to why some might consider **Oedipus** to be a good king.

_____
_____

8) Construct a brief **counterargument** as to why people might see **Oedipus** as a **morally bad** king.

_____
_____
_____

9) Rationalize how it might not be the fault of **Oedipus** for the killing of his father **Laius** and the marrying his mother **Jocasta**.

_____
_____
_____

10) Analyze how the play of <u>Oedipus Rex</u> by **Sophocles** is driven by a **plot** that relies heavily on **irony**.

_____
_____
_____

11) Explain how the awareness of the **audience** as to what will happen during the **play** <u>Oedipus Rex</u> has helped to add to its success over the **millennia**.

_____
_____
_____

12) Defend how the **search for truth** inside of <u>Oedipus Rex</u> can be seen as right, just, and brave regardless of the **plot** of a son **killing his father** and **marrying his mother**.

_____
_____
_____

13) Do YOU think **Oedipus** could have escaped his **fate**? Why or why not?

_____
_____
_____

Name_____

Period_____

Date_____

Ghosts, Murder, and More Murder: Hamlet Part 1: Crash Course English Literature #12

1) Provide a brief **background** that explains both the **vision** and **setting** for the play <u>Hamlet</u> (1599-1602) by William Shakespeare (1564-1616).

_____

_____

_____

_____

_____

_____

_____

2) Briefly analyze the **plot** of the story of <u>The Life of Amleth</u> (1208) by Saxo Grammaticus (1160-1220) and explain how it relates to William Shakespeare's <u>Hamlet</u>.

_____

_____

_____

_____

_____

_____

_____

_____

3) Evaluate whether YOU think that the changes made to **Hamlet** from the original story of <u>The Life of Amleth</u> make the story of <u>Hamlet</u> better or worse.

_____

_____

_____

_____

_____

_____

_____

_____

4) Analyze the effectiveness of the **dramatic shift** in the play <u>Hamlet</u> where **Hamlet** accidentally stabs **Polonius** rather than the intended victim, his uncle **Claudius**.

_____

_____

_____

_____

_____

_____

_____

_____

5) Analyze the line, "all's ill here about my heart," in **Act V Scene ii** of <u>Hamlet</u> that occurs at **Elsinore Castle** right before the **duel** between **Laertes** and **Hamlet**. *Clarify how it foreshadows the outcome of the fight.*

_____

_____

_____

6) Analyze the **foreshadowing** uttered during the fight scene in <u>Hamlet</u> where **King Claudius** murmurs," It is the poison'd cup: it is too late," (V.ii.235).

_____

_____

_____

_____

7) Draw conclusions as to why **King Claudius** searches for enemies that the **Elsinore Castle** can go to war with. *Then relate that to the war going on within his own home.*

_____

_____

_____

_____

_____

_____

8) Describe the comic relief **Rosencrantz** and **Guildenstern** provide in play <u>Hamlet</u>.

_____

_____

_____

_____

_____

9) Evaluate what was more damaging to **Hamlet**'s **character**, his **indecisiveness** or his **narcissism**.

_____

_____

_____

_____

_____

10) Analyze how the play <u>Hamlet</u> can be read as a **commentary** on **Shakespeare**'s own **environment** in **England**.

_____

_____

_____

_____

_____

11) Explain how **doubling** and **mirroring** play an important role in the **theme** of people being **able to change** inside of the world of Hamlet.

_____
_____
_____
_____
_____
_____
_____

12) Critique how Hamlet's **character** changes somewhat after he returns home from all of his **pirate adventures** away from **Elsinore Castle**.

_____
_____
_____
_____
_____
_____
_____

13) Analyze how the **words** and **actions** of **Ophelia**'s **character** can be seen a **subversive** double for **Hamlet** inside of the play Hamlet by William Shakespeare.

_____
_____
_____
_____
_____
_____
_____

14) Clarify the reasons as to why the **ghost** of **Hamlet's father** keeps haunting **Elsinore**. _Cite passages from Hamlet to defend your answer._

_____
_____
_____
_____
_____
_____

15) Describe how **earthly justice** has been **corrupted** inside of Hamlet.

_____
_____
_____
_____
_____
_____

Ophelia, Gertrude, and Regicide: Hamlet II: Crash Course English Literature #13

1) Analyze the problems that the character of **Hamlet** seems to have when **addressing women** inside of the play <u>Hamlet</u> (1599-1602) by William Shakespeare (1564-1616). *Cite evidence from the play <u>Hamlet</u> to defend your answer.*

_____

_____

_____

_____

_____

_____

_____

2) Compare the amount of **power** the **main characters** have in relationship to each other in the play <u>Hamlet</u>.

_____

_____

_____

_____

3) Analyze **Queen Gertrude**'s explanation about the death of **Ophelia** in **Act IV Scene vii** of <u>Hamlet</u>. *Cite evidence from the play <u>Hamlet</u> to defend your answer.*

_____

_____

_____

_____

_____

4) Evaluate the **psychological** problems experienced by **Ophelia** as a result of the accidental death of her father **Polonius** at the hands of **Hamlet**.

_____

_____

_____

_____

5) Analyze the **madness** experienced by **Ophelia** at the end of Act IV in <u>Hamlet</u> where she hands out **flowers** she has collected to **Claudius**, **Gertrude**, and **Laertes**.

_____

_____

_____

_____

6) Examine and report as to how **Ophelia** holds her own judgement on her body and ultimately her **death** after **Hamlet** kills her father and leaves **Elsinore Castle**.

_____
_____
_____
_____

7) Analyze how **Hamlet** sees his mother **Gertrude**'s marriage to his uncle **Claudius**.

_____
_____
_____
_____
_____
_____

8) Analyze where **Gertrude**'s **loyalties** lie. *Cite evidence from the play to show where her **allegiance** lies; to either her husband **Claudius** or to her son **Hamlet**.*

_____
_____
_____
_____
_____
_____

9) Make a case for which **character** in Hamlet YOU think is most **heroic**.

_____
_____
_____
_____
_____
_____

10) Examine and report on how **Hamlet** has changed throughout the course of the play in regards to his **mortality** by the beginning of the fifth act of the play Hamlet.

_____
_____
_____
_____
_____

11) Analyze the factors that cause **Hamlet** to go on a murderous **killing spree** at the end of the play Hamlet.

_____
_____
_____
_____
_____

Don't Reanimate Corpses! Frankenstein Part 1: Crash Course Literature 205

1) Explain why the opening **narrative** of the story of <u>Frankenstein</u> (1817) by Mary Shelly (1797-1851) is surprising to many readers.

_____
_____
_____
_____
_____
_____

2) Analyze how the novel <u>Frankenstein</u> by **Mary Shelly** affords the reader a **novel** (adj.) look at an **opening scene** in a **novel** (n.) that begins in the form of letters from the Arctic. (triple-threat **genre**: **science fiction, horror, romantic**)

_____
_____
_____
_____
_____
_____

3) Evaluate the life of author **Mary Shelly** and relate how her life may have influenced her to write the novel <u>Frankenstein</u> set in an **English Victorian society**.

_____
_____
_____
_____
_____
_____

4) Hypothesize how a dream by **Mary Shelly** was transformed by **romantic** ideas of **horror** and **awe** which in turn inspired the novel <u>Frankenstein</u>.

_____
_____
_____
_____
_____

5) Explain how **main character** in <u>Frankenstein</u>, scientist **Victor Frankenstein**, became obsessed with **reanimating** the dead.

_____
_____
_____
_____
_____

6) Draw conclusions as to why **Victor Frankenstein** freaks out and runs away after he **reanimates** a **corpse**.

_____
_____
_____
_____
_____

7) Explain the factors which caused the **reanimated corpse**, aka **Frankenstein**, to turn into a monster.

_____
_____
_____
_____
_____
_____
_____

8) Analyze the **theme** of **creation** which underlines the novel of Frankenstein. *Be sure to evaluate the origins of Frankenstein along with the story of the* **Greek Titan Prometheus**.

_____
_____
_____
_____
_____
_____
_____

9) Develop a logical argument as to how Frankenstein is a novel about when humans overstep their **boundaries**.

_____
_____
_____
_____
_____

10) Compare how Frankenstein borrows ideas from Paradise Lost (1667) by **John Milton** (1608-1674) with the similarities surrounding the role **free will** plays in understanding how **theology** affects one's actions inside of the universe.

_____
_____
_____
_____
_____

Frankenstein Part 2: Crash Course Literature 206

1) Clarify the difference between the **Romantics** and **romantics**.

_____
_____
_____
_____

2) Analyze how the **Romanticism** in the **Romantic Era** (1800-1850) championed **idealization** of **emotion** and **individualism** shaping both the art and literature of the 18th and 19th centuries.

_____
_____
_____
_____

3) Evaluate how somebody could see the novel Frankenstein (1818) by Mary Shelly (1797-1851) as a critique of **Romanticism**.

_____
_____
_____
_____

4) Evaluate how somebody could see the novel Frankenstein partly as an **autobiography** of the life of **Mary Shelly**.

_____
_____
_____
_____

5) Briefly explain what the term **intentional fallacy** means when it comes to literary theory.

_____
_____
_____

6) Explain the how the **character** of **Victor Frankenstein** may not like **women** and why he can be seen as **misogynistic**. *Cite an example from the novel to back up your claim.*

_____
_____
_____
_____

7) Why do YOU think that **Mary Shelley** would choose to display **women** as a **passive** and **collective group** that was doomed to a **life of suffering** inside of the novel Frankenstein?

_____
_____
_____
_____

8) Explain how somebody could read into Frankenstein as a novel that portrays **men** who fear, distrust, and **devalue women** so much so as to reproduce without them.

_____
_____
_____
_____
_____

9) Clarify the reasons why YOU think the novel Frankenstein has survived so long as part of the must-read section of the **English canon** of **literature**.

_____
_____
_____
_____

10) Connect scientists such as **Erasmus Darwin** (1731-1802) and **Luigi Galvani** (1737-1798) to the narrative of deeper meaning found inside of Frankenstein by **Mary Shelly**.

_____
_____
_____
_____
_____

11) Examine and then explain the **selfishness** of **Victor Frankenstein** in his creation of the monster **Frankenstein** and link that with his desire to **reanimate** dead **corpses**.

_____
_____
_____
_____

12) Evaluate how and why the novel of **Frankenstein** might be helpful in understanding the **morality** around blending the **surrounding technology** into the **social order** today.

_____
_____
_____
_____

Reader, it's Jane Eyre: Crash Course Literature 207

1) Evaluate the reasons why <u>Jane Eyre</u> (1847), by Victorian writer **Charlotte Bronte** (1816-1855), was seen as **scandalous** even though **Queen Victoria** (1819-1901) liked the novel.

_____
_____
_____
_____
_____
_____
_____
_____

2) Briefly analyze how the life of **Charlotte Bronte** inspired her to write the novel <u>Jane Eyre</u> during the **Victorian Era** (1837-1901) in **England**.

_____
_____
_____
_____
_____
_____

3) Draw conclusions as to why **Charlotte Bronte** and her sisters decided to writer under **male pseudonyms** rather than publishing **novels** under their own names.

_____
_____
_____
_____
_____
_____
_____

4) Critique how the **synopsis** of <u>Jane Eyre</u>, which ultimately ends with the unlikely marriage of **Jane Eyre** and **Mr. Rochester**, moves the book along with its twists and turns of **plot**.

_____
_____
_____
_____
_____
_____
_____
_____

5) Differentiate between the different types of **literary genres** which can be found in <u>Jane Eyre</u>. *Cite popular **critics** of the time or **passages** from the book <u>Jane Eyre</u> to defend your answer. According to....*

a) **Autobiography**

_____
_____
_____
_____
_____

b) **Bildungsroman**

_____
_____
_____
_____
_____
_____

c) **Romantic and Gothic**

_____
_____
_____
_____
_____
_____

d) **Detective**

_____
_____
_____
_____
_____
_____

6) Analyze how the combination of **seriousness** and **psychological realism** expressed inside the novel of <u>Jane Eyre</u> by **Charlotte Bronte** contribute to its success as a **novel**.

_____
_____
_____
_____
_____
_____
_____
_____

Name_____

Period_____

Date_____

If One Finger Brought Oil- Things Fall Apart part 1: Crash Course Literature 208

1) Evaluate the reasons why the novel <u>Things Fall Apart</u> (1958) by Chinua Achebe (1930-2018), which takes place in **Nigeria** during the late **colonial period** in **Africa** during the **19th century**, is such an important English novel. *Cite an example from the novel to defend your answer.*

_____
_____
_____
_____
_____
_____
_____
_____
_____
_____

2) Differentiate between the both the **outside pressures** of **colonialism** and the **interior pressures** of the main character **Okonkwo** in the **opening paragraph** of the novel <u>Things Fall Apart</u>.

_____
_____
_____
_____
_____

3) Analyze the meaning of the line, "red in tooth and claw," from <u>Things Fall Apart</u> which has its origins in *In Memoriam A.H.H. (1850)* by **Alfred Lord Tennyson** (1809-1892).

_____
_____
_____
_____
_____

4) Cite evidence that defends **Okonkwo**'s reasons for "pouncing," on people inside of <u>Things Fall Apart</u> by Chinua Achebe, and then explain the quote YOU chose.

_____
_____
_____
_____
_____
_____
_____

5) Critique **Okonkwo**'s world in <u>Things Fall Apart</u> by **Chinua Achebe** by comparing it to the Greek world in <u>Oedipus Rex</u> (430 BCE) by **Sophocles** (496-406 BCE).

_____

_____

_____

_____

_____

6) Draw conclusions as to why **Ikemefuna** had to be turned over to another clan as a **sacrifice** for the benefit of **Okonkwo's clan** inside of the novel <u>Things Fall Apart</u>.

_____

_____

_____

_____

7) Connect the reasons why **Okonkwo** was ultimately **exiled** from his **village** inside of <u>Things Fall Apart</u> and then show how this connects to **Okonkwo**'s avoidance of all things female.

_____

_____

_____

_____

8) Clarify why **Okonkwo** not only needed to be banished from his **village** but also from all **communal** memory.

_____

_____

_____

_____

9) Analyze what happens in the relationship between **Okonkwo** and his teenage son **Nwoye** in <u>Things Fall Apart</u> as a result of the **clash of cultures** between **Africans** and **Europeans.**

_____

_____

_____

_____

_____

10) Draw conclusions as to why **Okonkwo's eyes** never really get opened inside of <u>Things Fall Apart</u> by Chinua Achebe.

_____

_____

_____

Name_____
Period_____
Date_____

Things Fall Apart, Part 2: Crash Course Literature 209

1) Evaluate the **historical context** surrounding the **colonization of Africa** during the 19th century inside of the story Things Fall Apart (1958) written by **Chinua Achebe (1930-2013)**.

_____
_____
_____
_____
_____

2) Examine and explain how Chinua Achebe's **childhood** set him up to be a perfect **conduit** between the **Igbo** and **English cultures** in order to create the novel Things Fall Apart.

_____
_____
_____
_____
_____

3) Describe the reasons for the close **familial** ties between **Nigerian tribal men** and their ancestral. *Cite a passage from the novel Things Fall Apart to defend your answer.*

_____
_____
_____
_____
_____
_____

4) Explain why **British colonialism** didn't work for **Africans** who had lived in **Africa** for thousands of years.

_____
_____
_____
_____

5) Assess the **societal problems** which had already transformed many **African communities** in **Nigeria** by the end of the novel as a result of the new **British** government.

_____
_____
_____
_____

6) Defend why the **African colonies** were so popular with the **European nations**.

_____

_____

_____

_____

7) Why do YOU think that **European countries** advanced the ideas of spreading **commerce**, **Christianity**, and **civilization** to **African countries**?

_____

_____

_____

_____

8) Draw conclusions as to why the **British** were so obsessed with **Palm trees** in **West Africa** after the outlawing of the **slave trade** within the **British Empire**.

_____

_____

_____

_____

_____

9) Clarify the differences between missionaries **Mr. Kiaga**, **Mr. Brown**, and **James Smith**. _Be sure to clarify why missionary **James Smith** was so detested by the **people of Umofia**._

_____

_____

_____

_____

_____

10) Investigate the reasons why the **villagers** did NOT rally to the side of **Okonkwo** when he was organizing the villagers for a forceful resistance against the **British**. _Cite evidence from Things Fall Apart to defend your answer._

_____

_____

_____

_____

_____

11) Draw conclusions as to why the **loss of humanity** in the closing chapter of Things Fall Apart is largely due in part to the **colonization of Nigeria**.

_____

_____

_____

_____

Name_____

Period_____

Date_____

To Kill a Mockingbird Part 1: Crash Course Literature 210

1) Why do YOU think that the novel <u>To Kill a Mockingbird</u> (1960) by Harper Lee (1926-2016) was considered to be a novel of strong contemporary **national significance**? *Defend your answer with **thematic examples** from the novel.*

_____

_____

_____

_____

_____

_____

_____

2) Explain the simplicity of **tone** and **voice** inside the novel <u>To Kill a Mockingbird</u> (1960) when confronting powerful **social issues** in the **South** such as **race** and **gender**. *Cite examples from the novel to justify your answer.*

_____

_____

_____

_____

_____

_____

_____

_____

_____

3) Briefly analyze the parallels between **Harper Lee** and the **main character** Jean Louise **"Scout"** Finch in the novel <u>To Kill a Mockingbird</u>.

_____

_____

_____

_____

4) Explain how the **plot** of <u>To Kill a Mockingbird</u> by Harper Lee involving two children harmlessly sipping lemonade during the summertime in **Maycomb, Alabama** became twisted and intricately involved with the **fate** of their neighbor **Boo Radley**.

_____

_____

_____

_____

_____

5) Analyze the **hallmarks** of the case of African-American **Tom Robinson** and his court appointed **public defender Atticus Finch**.

_____
_____
_____
_____
_____

6) Evaluate why it was important that **Scout** was challenged to look at things from another person's **perspective** in order to feel **empathy** inside of the novel <u>To Kill a Mockingbird</u>.

_____
_____
_____
_____
_____

7) Explain how **Boo Radley** was described as a **monster** at the beginning of the novel <u>To Kill a Mockingbird</u>, while **Jem**, **Scout**, and **Dill** were seen as his potential **victims**. _Cite examples from the novel to justify your claims._

_____
_____
_____
_____
_____
_____

8) Cite evidence from the novel <u>To Kill A Mockingbird</u> that shows how **Scout**'s father **Atticus** was seen as a **heroic knight**.

_____
_____
_____
_____
_____
_____

9) Show how **ignorance**, **racism**, and **violence** turn out to be the real **monsters** in the novel <u>To Kill a Mockingbird</u>. _Cite examples from the novel to justify your claims._

_____
_____
_____
_____
_____
_____

Race, Class, and Gender in To Kill a Mockingbird: Crash Course Literature 211

1) Critique **class structure** in relation to the **common perceptions** of **race, class,** and **gender** in the **Southern United States** during the **1950s** as seen inside of the book To Kill a Mockingbird (1960) by **Harper Lee** (1926-2016).

_____
_____
_____
_____
_____
_____
_____

2) Analyze the reasons why **Scout,** the **main character** in To Kill a Mockingbird, was confused by the hatred and violence she experiences in **Maycomb, Alabama.** *Cite a passage from To Kill A Mockingbird in order to defend your answer.*

_____
_____
_____
_____
_____
_____
_____

3) Evaluate how **Scout** was able to disperse the crowd that was converging on the jail to lynch **Tom** with the help of **Mr. Cunningham.** *Include the role that African-American housekeeper Calpurnia plays in influencing Scout's morality in your answer.*

_____
_____
_____
_____
_____
_____

4) Analyze how **Calpurnia** epitomizes the **double-life** many **African Americans** in the **1950s** were forced to play as a consequence of their **race.** *Include reference to the The Souls of Black Folk (1903) by W.E.B. Du Bois (1868-1963) in your answer.*

_____
_____
_____
_____
_____
_____

5) Evaluate how **Southern femininity** plays a strong **ideological role** in the life of **Calpurnia** in regards to **Scout**, her **church**, and her **community**.

_____

_____

_____

_____

_____

_____

_____

6) Develop a logical argument to explain the reasons for the harrowing experience **Tom Robinson** faced inside of **Maycomb, Alabama.** *Include what he went through after being falsely accused of committing a crime and sentenced to death due to his race.*

_____

_____

_____

_____

_____

_____

7) Explain how the **actions** of **Atticus Finch** towards **Mrs. Dubose**, **Tom Robinson**, and **Bob Ewell** serve as an example of his type of **anti-racist** and pacifist **character**.

_____

_____

_____

_____

_____

_____

_____

_____

_____

8) Why do YOU think the title of the book To Kill a Mockingbird is To Kill a Mockingbird and not something else? *Defend your answer citing examples from the text.*

_____

_____

_____

_____

_____

_____

_____

_____

_____

_____

Aliens, Time Travel, and Dresden-Slaughterhouse-Five Part 1: Crash Course Literature 212

1) Examine how the **setting** of the novel <u>Slaughterhouse-Five</u> (1969) by Kurt Vonnegut (1922-2007) about bombing of **Dresden, Germany** during **World War II** (1939-1945) adds to its status as an **anti-war novel**.

_____

_____

_____

_____

_____

_____

2) Outline the **non-linear events** that occur to the **protagonist** and main character **Billy Pilgrim** inside of the novel <u>Slaughterhouse-Five</u> by Kurt Vonnegut.

_____

_____

_____

_____

_____

_____

_____

_____

_____

_____

_____

3) Evaluate whether or not YOU think that the **logic** behind the **narrative** of **Billy Pilgrim** is made perfectly clear inside of the novel <u>Slaughterhouse-Five</u> by Kurt Vonnegut.

_____

_____

_____

_____

_____

4) Analyze how the **first** and **last chapters** of Kurt Vonnegut's <u>Slaughterhouse-Five</u> were aided by his own experiences during **World War II** (1939-1945). *Include why YOU think Vonnegut chooses to inform the reader that they are reading a novel.*

_____

_____

_____

_____

_____

5) Draw conclusions as to the effect the **fire-bombing** of **Dresden**, Germany in 1945 had on not only on its own **civilian population** but also the **prisoners of war** held there during **World War 2** (1939-1945).

_____

_____

_____

_____

_____

_____

6) Explain the **literary effect** the reader experiences as a result of Kurt Vonnegut's **non-confrontational** description of the **firebombing** of **Dresden** rather than writing about the destruction in detail. *(Cite evidence from the novel to defend your answer.)*

_____

_____

_____

_____

_____

_____

7) Analyze why Kurt Vonnegut would choose to have **Billy Pilgrim** shy away from talking about the destruction of **Dresden** inside of Slaughterhouse-Five.

_____

_____

_____

_____

_____

8) Analyze the **absurdity** of using a barber shop **metaphor** to represent the **guards** in Chapter 8 of Slaughterhouse-Five by Kurt Vonnegut.

_____

_____

_____

_____

_____

9) Examine Chapter 1 of Slaughterhouse-Five and report why **Kurt Vonnegut** thought it would be easy for him to describe the **bombing of Dresden**. *(Cite evidence from the novel to defend your answer.)*

_____

_____

_____

_____

_____

_____

PTSD and Alien Abduction-Slaughterhouse-Five Part 2: Crash Course Literature 213

1) Explain the reasons why YOU think main character **Billy Pilgrim** suffers from **PTSD** (Post Traumatic Stress Disorder) as narrated in a string of **flashbacks** inside the novel <u>Slaughterhouse-Five</u> (1969) by Kurt Vonnegut (1922-2007).

_____
_____
_____
_____
_____
_____
_____

2) Compare how the philosophy of the **Tralfamadorian aliens** aid **Billy Pilgrim** in coming to terms with the shame and horror of his treatment by the **Germans** during **World War II** (1939-1945).

_____
_____
_____
_____
_____

3) Analyze the opening line, "All this happened, more or less," in <u>Slaughterhouse-Five</u> by Kurt Vonnegut to show how the story recounted by **Billy Pilgrim** after the **fire-bombing** of **Dresden** is an excellent example of **revisionism**.

_____
_____
_____
_____
_____
_____

4) Clarify how the use of **revisionism** inside of <u>Slaughterhouse-Five</u> by Kurt Vonnegut portrays the necessary steps taken along the journey to recovery from **PTSD**.

_____
_____
_____
_____
_____
_____

5) Explain how the **Tralfamadorian aliens** view the concept of **time** and **space**.

_____
_____
_____
_____

6) Compare <u>Slaughterhouse-Five</u> to the ancient **Greek play** <u>Oedipus Rex</u> (441 BCE).

_____
_____
_____
_____
_____

7) Morally justify **decisions** made by **Billy Pilgrim** throughout the novel <u>Slaughterhouse-Five</u>. _Defend your answer with examples._

_____
_____
_____
_____
_____
_____

8) Weigh the concepts of **free will** and **moral responsibility** reflected in the **structure** of <u>Slaughterhouse-Five</u> by Kurt Vonnegut.

_____
_____
_____
_____
_____
_____

9) Explain the reasons why YOU think the **narrative** of <u>Slaughterhouse-Five</u> by Kurt Vonnegut jumps forward and backward in **time** and **space**.

_____
_____
_____
_____

10) Outline the reasons why <u>Slaughterhouse-Five</u> is like **Tralfamadorian literature**:
   a) _____
   b) _____
   c) _____

11) Evaluate how <u>Slaughterhouse-Five</u> is an example of an **anti-bildungsroman**.

_____
_____
_____

12) Evaluate the **statement**, "so it goes," by **Billy Pilgrim** in <u>Slaughterhouse-Five</u>.

_____
_____
_____

Slavery, Ghosts, and Beloved: Crash Course Literature 214

1) Analyze the ways in which **Nobel** prize winner Toni Morrison (1931-Present) writes the novel <u>Beloved</u> (1987) in order to better understand the lives of others who have been downtrodden on account of their history and **race**.

_____
_____
_____
_____
_____
_____
_____

2) Describe how the **character** of **Beloved** by Toni Morrison in the novel <u>Beloved</u> is both **beautiful** and **haunting**. *Defend your answer with a short quote from the novel <u>Beloved</u>.*

_____
_____
_____
_____
_____
_____

3) Briefly describe how **slaves** are portrayed inside of the novel <u>Beloved</u> by Toni Morrison.

_____
_____
_____
_____
_____
_____
_____

4) Investigate and briefly report on the **narrative power** of the **characters** of **Sethe** and **Baby Suggs** inside of the novel <u>Beloved</u> by Toni Morrison. *Include why their stories are so horrifying.*

_____
_____
_____
_____
_____
_____
_____

5) Explain how protagonist **Sethe** distributes her love between her daughter **Denver** and her lover **Paul D** inside the novel Beloved by Toni Morrison. *Include the advice **Paul D** gives to **Sethe** about how to raise her child.*

_____
_____
_____
_____
_____
_____
_____

6) Analyze how the institution of **slavery** destroyed the families of **slaves** in the **South**.

_____
_____
_____
_____
_____
_____
_____
_____

7) Evaluate the effectiveness of writing the novel <u>Beloved</u> from a number of different **perspectives**.

_____
_____
_____
_____
_____
_____
_____
_____

8) Draw conclusions as to why the novel <u>Beloved</u> ends on a hopeful note for the **characters** of **Denver, Paul D**, and **Sethe**.

_____
_____
_____
_____
_____
_____
_____

9) Explain how the novel <u>Beloved</u> is actually a **dialogue** with the **idea of America** itself.

_____
_____
_____
_____
_____

Name_____
Period_____
Date_____

Langston Hughes & the Harlem Renaissance: Crash Course Literature 215

1) Briefly analyze the **historical significance** of the **Harlem Renaissance** (1918-1935) which began just after the first **World War** (1914-1919) and lasted a few years into the **Great Depression** (1929-1939).

_____
_____
_____
_____
_____
_____

2) Analyze the novel <u>Souls of Black Folk</u> (1903) by **W.E.B. Dubois** (1868-1963) and explain its portrayal of the **double consciousness** inside of the **African American experience** during the **Harlem Renaissance**.

_____
_____
_____

3) Investigate the role **poetry** played inside the life of African American **Langston Hughes** (1902-1967) and then explain how his easily accessible and **familiar language** helped to connect his experiences with his readers.

_____
_____
_____
_____
_____

4) Clarify the reasons why **Langston Hughes** didn't write in a **classical format** or in the form of a **Shakespearean sonnet** when writing his **poetry**.

_____
_____
_____
_____

5) Analyze the essay *The Negro Artist and the Racial Mountain* (1926) by **Langston Hughes** and point out the problems Hughes had with other **black writers** of the time.

_____
_____
_____
_____
_____

6) Briefly analyze James Baldwin's (1924-1987) **critique** on the writings of Langston Hughes.

_____

_____

_____

7) Evaluate the effectiveness of the **imagery** inside of the **poem**, "The Negro Speaks of Rivers," (1920) by Langston Hughes.

_____

_____

_____

_____

8) Analyze how Langston Hughes pursues a **lyric mode** in his **poem**, "The Negro Speaks of Rivers," to create a type of **spiritual sermon**. _Include how he uses the **river** to connect himself to his **ancestors**._

_____

_____

_____

_____

_____

9) Analyze how Langston Hughes uses **language** inside of his **poem**, "The Negro Speaks of Rivers," to show how people actively participate in human life and act on their own accord.

_____

_____

_____

_____

_____

_____

10) Analyze how **Langston Hughes** uses **language** inside of his **poem**, "Harlem," (1951) to inspire **African Americans** to achieve the **American dream**.

_____

_____

_____

_____

11) Why do YOU think withholding **true equality** has real risks and real costs to everyone participating in the **human experience**?

_____

_____

_____

_____

The Poetry of Sylvia Plath: Crash Course Literature 216

1) Explain how some view **Silvia Plath** (1932-1963) as an avenger in support of **women's rights**. *Include why she is considered to be a **feminist** who wrote about **female inequality** before women achieved **equal rights**.*

_____
_____
_____
_____
_____
_____
_____
_____
_____
_____
_____

2) Analyze the **tone** inside the **poem**, "Cut," (1962) by Silvia Plath. *Cite examples from the poem, "Cut," to defend your answer.*

_____
_____
_____
_____
_____
_____
_____
_____
_____
_____

3) Evaluate how **society**, portrayed inside of The Bell Jar (1963) by Silvia Plath, attempts to deal with the **depression** of the **main character**.

_____
_____
_____
_____
_____
_____
_____
_____

4) Investigate and analyze the reasons surrounding the death of **Silvia Plath** in 1963.

_____
_____
_____
_____
_____
_____

5) Analyze the **social criticism** that blossoms into the brutality, anger, and morbidity found inside of one of Sylvia Plath's most famous poems, "Lady Lazarus," from her book of poems, Ariel (1965). *Cite examples from the poem "Lady Lazarus," to defend your answer.*

_____

_____

_____

_____

_____

6) Assess how **Sylvia Plath** uses **repetition** and **rhyme** inside of "Lady Lazarus," so that the **reader** is forced to stay inside of the poem.

_____

_____

_____

_____

_____

_____

7) Compare the **similarities** and **differences** between **Emily Dickinson** (1830-1886) and **Sylvia Plath**.

_____

_____

_____

_____

_____

_____

8) Connect how **Sylvia Plath** is seen as part of the **Confessional School of Poetry** along with **Robert Lowell** (1917-1977) and **Anne Sexton** (1928-1974).

_____

_____

_____

_____

_____

_____

_____

9) Analyze how **Sylvia Plath** uses **hospital tulips** to connect **humanity** with **hope** inside of the poem "Tulips" (1961).

_____

_____

_____

_____

Writing Counterarguments

Tip 10) **Tips and Tricks**

Writing a **counterargument** can be tricky as many times writing a counterargument asks the writer to try and think of the **opposite point of view** than the question asks or possibly champions the opposite of what YOU normally think. A counterargument takes into account the **opposing point of view** and explains it even if that viewpoint is at odds with the **original viewpoint** or YOUR point of view. Learning how to write a counterargument can vastly increase the quality of YOUR essay as both points of view are given time for reflection and thought, and can prove instrumental in swaying the opinions of others. Counterarguments have the power to **empathize** with another person's **point of view** bringing an opposing viewpoint into your essay and grounding your reader's expectations prior to explaining why YOUR point of view is possibly correct. Also try not to state the words, "in my opinion," anywhere in your essay. YOUR opinion should be apparent throughout the essay without that crutch. Try and remain in a neutral 3rd person writing technique when writing your essay. Steer away from first as well as second person words that include possessive pronouns such as "I" or "you," or "your." Lastly, challenge yourself to steer away from "TH" words especially at the beginning of a sentence like, "the," or "this," or "these," or "those," or "them."

CASE EXAMPLE #1 The Death Penalty:

a) Take for example your views on the death penalty when understanding the nature of a **counterargument**. When writing a counterargument for the death penalty, you also need a strong argument to force you away from being neutral regardless of if you are **apathetic** on the death penalty and wish not to pick a side. In an argument you must pick a side. If you don't want to, do it just for practice and see what would happen if you liked this or that. The nature of the argument needs one to pick a side. In the argument and counterargument essay scenario, you have two choices in what to believe. YOU can choose to either be **pro** (for the) death penalty or **anti** (against) the death penalty. There is no middle ground if you wish to write a good essay.

b) If YOU are for the death penalty (aka pro death penalty) than your argument should back up YOUR ideas as to why **state sanctioned killing** should be permissible. If the individual deserves to be put to death, then YOUR argument could range everywhere from cost of **incarceration** to the punishment fits the crime type of argument.

c) If YOU are against the **death penalty** than your argument should include why it is wrong for the state to kill an individual. YOUR argument may range everywhere from a **theological** point of view to YOUR view of **morality**, or what is right or wrong, and why nobody not even the state should be allowed to kill a human being.

d) A counterargument is not friends with a middle of the road point of view and this point of view should be avoided when writing a counterargument, no matter how **blasé** your point of view may be on the **death penalty**. Take a stand and defend your answer and then explain why the other side has a valid point of view before blowing that argument out of the water with your better and stronger point of view! Only the strongest arguments survive yet **empathy** is key to convincing others you are correct!

Their Eyes Were Watching God: Crash Course Literature 301

1) Why do YOU think it can be important to take in as many **different perspectives** as possible when trying to learn to **read critically**?

_____

_____

_____

_____

_____

2) According to her **autobiography**, why did **Zora Neale Hurston** (1891-1960) write the novel Their Eyes Were Watching God (1937)?

_____

_____

_____

_____

3) Examine how the book Their Eyes Were Watching God is actually a mixture of a couple of different **genres**. *Provide examples of how the book is an example of each genre.*
   a) **Bildungsroman**:

   _____

   _____

   _____

   b) **Romance (Tea Cake)**:

   _____

   _____

4) Critique what the critic **Richard Wright** (1908-1960) didn't understand after reading the novel Their Eyes Were Watching God.

_____

_____

_____

_____

_____

5) Evaluate how the novel Their Eyes Were Watching God is really about **main character** Janie's **emancipation**.

_____

_____

_____

_____

_____

6) Taking the **counterargument** into consideration, explain how the novel <u>Their Eyes Were Watching God</u> is NOT about **main character** Janie's **emancipation**.

_____

_____

_____

_____

_____

7) Draw conclusions as to why **Hurston** would choose to write <u>Their Eyes Were Watching God</u> in a **colloquial style** using **vernacular speech** and **nonstandard spelling**. _Cite examples in your answers along with your explanations._

_____

_____

_____

_____

_____

_____

_____

_____

_____

8) Provide a **short analysis** of the differences between the three men with whom **Janie** has a **romantic relationship** with inside the novel <u>Their Eyes Were Watching God</u>.
   a) **Logan**:

   _____

   _____

   _____

   b) **Joe Starks**:

   _____

   _____

   _____

   c) **Tea Cake**:

   _____

   _____

   _____

9) Analyze the **self-realization** and **empowerment** experienced by **main character Janie** in relation to her **character arc** in the novel <u>Their Eyes Were Watching God</u> by **Zora Neale Hurston**.

_____

_____

_____

_____

Name_____

Period_____

Date_____

The Adventures of Huckleberry Finn Part 1: Crash Course Literature 302

1) Examine and report how the **early life** of Samuel Langhorne Clemens, aka **Mark Twain** (1835-1910) author of <u>The Adventures of Huckleberry Finn</u> (1884), **influenced** the **setting** for his stories along the **Mississippi River**.

_____

_____

_____

_____

2) Briefly compare the **differences** between the novels <u>The Adventures of Tom Sawyer</u> (1876) and <u>The Adventures of Huckleberry Finn</u> written by **Mark Twain**.

_____

_____

_____

_____

_____

3) Analyze why the **character** of **Huckleberry Finn** chooses to try and become **civilized** inside of the novel <u>The Adventures of Huckleberry Finn</u> by **Mark Twain**.

_____

_____

_____

_____

_____

_____

_____

4) Develop a logical argument as to why **Huckleberry Finn** fakes his own **death** and runs away to live on a **river island**.

_____

_____

_____

_____

5) Evaluate the **models of adulthood** that **Huckleberry Finn** runs away from in order to live on a **river island**.

_____

_____

_____

_____

_____

6) Draw conclusions as to why **Huckleberry Finn** develops a **conscience** and chooses to hide the black runaway **adult** slave **Jim** whom he meets on the **river island**.

_____
_____
_____
_____
_____
_____

7) Describe the **irony** of **Tom Sawyer's plan** to win **Jim** his **freedom**.

_____
_____
_____
_____
_____
_____

8) Critique the **backlash** that occurred soon after the **publication** of The Adventures of Huckleberry Finn by **Mark Twain** due to its confluence of ideas in **plot**, **style**, and **language** surrounding the idea of **slavery**.

_____
_____
_____
_____
_____
_____

9) Evaluate the **significance** of book The Adventures of Huckleberry Finn as a great American novel by analyzing the **unusual relationship** between the **characters** of **Huckleberry Finn** and the "escaped" slave **Jim**.

_____
_____
_____
_____
_____
_____
_____

10) Analyze the **language** that **Mark Twain** uses to describe **Jim** in the novel The Adventures of Huckleberry Finn.

_____
_____
_____
_____
_____
_____

The Raft, the River, and The Weird Ending of Huckleberry Finn: Crash Course Literature 303

1) Show how the **Mississippi River** serves as a **metaphor** for the **plot** of unfolding events inside the novel <u>The Adventures of Huckleberry Finn</u> (1884) by **Mark Twain** (1835-1910). *Cite evidence from the novel to defend your answer.*

_____
_____
_____
_____
_____
_____
_____

2) Evaluate the **arguments** surrounding <u>The Adventures of Huckleberry Finn</u> by critics **Lionel Trilling** (1905-1975) and **T.S. Eliot** (1888-1965) both whom point out that the **serenity** of the **river** is seen in contrast to the **violence** on **land**.

_____
_____
_____
_____
_____
_____
_____
_____

3) Analyze the **idea of freedom** that is championed by **Mark Twain** inside of the novel <u>The Adventures of Huckleberry Finn</u>. *Cite an example from the book to defend your answer.*

_____
_____
_____
_____
_____
_____
_____

4) What do YOU think **Mark Twain** is arguing for and against inside of the book <u>The Adventures of Huckleberry Finn</u>? *Defend your answer with examples.*

_____
_____
_____
_____
_____
_____

5) Analyze the significance of Huckleberry Finn **romanticizing** the **raft** inside of <u>The Adventures of Huckleberry Finn</u>. *Cite an example from the book to defend your answer.*

_____

_____

_____

_____

_____

6) Differentiate the **irony** surrounding the **idea of freedom** that the **river island** is both a **paradise** and a **problem** inside the novel <u>The Adventures of Huckleberry Finn</u>.

_____

_____

_____

_____

7) Draw conclusions as to how **true freedom**, **loyalty**, and **friendship** are portrayed inside the **character arcs** of the **characters** in the novel <u>The Adventures of Huckleberry Finn</u>.

_____

_____

_____

_____

_____

8) Investigate the **satirical complications** that **Tom** and **Huck** experience during the carrying out of their twisted **escape plan** to free the already free former slave **Jim**.

_____

_____

_____

_____

9) Assess the **character arc** of **Huckleberry Finn**. Show how he has learned to **appreciate life** and to be nice to others by the end of the novel <u>The Adventures of Huckleberry Finn</u>.

_____

_____

_____

_____

_____

10) Do YOU believe that **racial injustice** continued after the **Civil War** (1861-1865) and the passage of the **13th**, **14th**, and **15th Amendments**? Why or why not? Defend your answer.

_____

_____

_____

_____

Shakespeare's Sonnets: Crash Course Literature 304

1) Investigate the **rhyme schemes** of **Shakespearean stanzas** mastered by **William Shakespeare** (1564-1616) in his book Shakespeare's Sonnets (1609).

_____
_____
_____
_____
_____
_____

2) Investigate and report on the history of the **English sonnet**.

_____
_____
_____
_____

3) Evaluate the timeless success of the **publication** of Shakespeare's Sonnets.

_____
_____
_____

4) Show how Shakespeare's Sonnets placed an emphasis on the importance of poetry in order to convey feelings of **everlasting love** captured inside of Sonnet 55. *Cite a stanza from Sonnet 55 to defend your answer.*

_____
_____
_____
_____
_____
_____
_____

5) Analyze the **extended metaphor** of **fair youth** coming undone by **time and death** in Sonnet 18, "Shall I Compare Thee to a Summer's Day," by William Shakespeare.

_____
_____
_____
_____
_____

6) Analyze how the poet in Sonnet 116, "Let Me Not to the Marriage of True Minds Admit Impediment," defines **true love** as love that always perseveres.

_____
_____
_____
_____
_____
_____

7) Analyze how **female beauty** is upended in Sonnet 130, "My Mistress's Eyes Are Nothing Like the Sun," along with how the poet shows what it is like to love a woman with **physical shortcomings**.

_____
_____
_____
_____
_____
_____
_____

8) Evaluate the **Elizabethan idea** that **human life is temporary** but **poetry is forever** factoring in the **high mortality rate** at the time.

_____
_____
_____
_____
_____

9) Analyze the line, "love is not time's fool," in Sonnet 116, and analyze the reasons why a person might choose to read these lines of poetry at a **wedding**.

_____
_____
_____
_____
_____
_____

10) Analyze the twist in the **final couplet** of Sonnet 130 where the poet **humanizes** the **dark lady** in the line, "And yet by heaven I think my love is rare/As any she belied on false compare."

_____
_____
_____
_____

Lord of the Flies: Crash Course Literature 305

1) Analyze how the life of **William Golding** (1911-1993) and his service in the **Navy** during **World War II** (1939-1945) inspired him to write Lord of the Flies (1954).

_____

_____

_____

_____

_____

2) Hypothesize as to why the **boys** in the Lord of the Flies were flying over a **desert island** before their plane was shot down.

_____

_____

_____

3) Evaluate why YOU think the **plot** of Lord of the Flies includes the killing of **Simon** by a bunch of **choir boys** led by a kid named **Jack**.

_____

_____

_____

_____

_____

4) Explain how Lord of the Flies could be grouped inside the same **genre, Robinsonade,** same as the books Robinson Crusoe (1719) by Daniel Dafoe (1660-1731) and Coral Island (1858) by R.M. Ballantyne (1825-1894).

_____

_____

_____

_____

_____

_____

5) Analyze how the **dangers** inside the novel Lord of the Flies aren't **external** but **internal**.

_____

_____

_____

_____

_____

_____

_____

6) Compare how **William Golding's views** of the **social order** inside of the Lord of the Flies are more in tandem with the thinking of **Thomas Hobbes** (1588-1679) than **Jean-Jacques Rousseau** (1712-1788).

_____
_____
_____
_____
_____
_____

7) Analyze the **imagery** William Golding uses in his **depiction** of civilization's descent into **savagery** inside of the novel Lord of the Flies.

_____
_____
_____
_____
_____
_____

8) Analyze how the **theme** of savagery ties in with the **scar** and the **beastie** on the **island**.

_____
_____
_____
_____
_____

9) Explain what **Simon**'s relationship is with the **Lord of the Flies** (aka rotting pig head).

_____
_____
_____
_____
_____

10) Why do YOU think that **Ralph** and **Piggy** resist becoming members of **Jack's gang**?

_____
_____
_____
_____

11) Briefly assess how it could be seen that Lord of the Flies is playing out **fears** and **fantasies** of **masculinity**.

_____
_____
_____
_____

100 Years of Solitude Part 1: Crash Course Literature 306

1) Analyze how the life of **Gabriel Garcia Marquez** (1927-2014) inspired him to write the **multigenerational story** of 100 Years of Solitude (1967) set in the **fictional** Colombian town of **Macondo**.

_____
_____
_____
_____
_____

2) Clarify why **Gabriel Garcia Marquez** uses **name repetition** throughout the **generations** to describe the **personalities** of the **Aurelianos** and the **José Arcadios** inside of 100 Years of Solitude.

_____
_____
_____
_____
_____

3) Explain the reasons why many people see the novel One Hundred Years of Solitude as both a masterpiece of **magical realism** and **experimental fiction**.

_____
_____
_____
_____
_____
_____

4) Analyze how **Gabriel Garcia Marquez** plays around with **time** in the novel 100 Years of Solitude to show the reader the **past**, **present**, and **future** simultaneously.

_____
_____
_____
_____
_____

5) Draw conclusions as to how **individual perspectives** influence the **idea of history** inside of the book 100 Years of Solitude.

_____
_____
_____
_____
_____

6) Explain **phenomena** in terms of concepts utilizing the idea of **magical realism** when ice is discovered in the novel <u>100 Years of Solitude</u>.

_____

_____

_____

_____

_____

7) Clarify the advantage of placing the novel <u>100 Years of Solitude</u> inside of multiple **realities**, as well as inside of multiple **generations** and **perspectives** of the **Buendía Family**.

_____

_____

_____

_____

_____

8) Develop a logical argument as to the reasons why **magical realism** does away with the **exposition**, **linear time structure**, and **certainty** many readers expect when they read a novel.

_____

_____

_____

_____

_____

9) Connect how **Gabriel Garcia Marquez** utilizes the straightforward **tone** of the **narrator** to hold together the many **vignettes** inside of <u>100 Years of Solitude</u> as well as to confront the violence occurring throughout the novel.

_____

_____

_____

_____

_____

10) Analyze how the **Sanskrit parchments** of the gypsy **Melquíades** not only predict the entire history of the **Buendía family**, but also mirror the, "predictions in coded lines of poetry," inside of the novel <u>100 Years of Solitude</u>.

_____

_____

_____

_____

_____

_____

100 Years of Solitude Part 2: Crash Course Literature 307

1) Develop a logical argument as to how the **multigenerational** story of <u>100 Years of Solitude</u> (1967) by **Gabriel Garcia Marquez** (1927-2014) can be read as a **fictionalized history** of **Latin America**'s struggle with **colonialism**.

_____

_____

_____

_____

_____

2) Clarify why many historians consider **banana republics** to be examples of **exploitative neocolonialism**. *(*banana republics=any unstable Latin American country whose economy is tied to one product such as bananas)*

_____

_____

_____

_____

_____

3) Compare the similarities and differences between **colonialism** and **neocolonialism**.

_____

_____

_____

_____

_____

4) Why do YOU think people inside of **South American nations** such as **Columbia** would allow **businesses** from the **United States** to exploit the **natural resources** of their countries?

_____

_____

_____

_____

5) Connect how the life of **Gabriel Garcia Marquez** inspired him to write the **fictionalized history** of Latin America's struggle with **colonialism**. *Defend your answer by including real life events such as the **Banana Strike Massacre** (1926).*

_____

_____

_____

_____

_____

6) Why do YOU think that the **lens of history** of what actually happened at a historical event, such as the **Banana Strike Massacre**, isn't always entirely **objective**?

_____

_____

_____

_____

7) Draw conclusions as to how **Gabriel Garcia Marquez** invokes **mythology** in order to provide **imaginary solutions** to **real social contradictions** inside of 100 Years of Solitude.

_____

_____

_____

_____

_____

8) Evaluate the **scientific reasoning** inured in arguments of the banana company's **lawyers** to justify the **terrible working conditions**, **unsanitary living quarters**, and **scrip money** used to dismiss the **claims** of the workers.

_____

_____

_____

_____

_____

9) Clarify the disconnect and dislocation from the **plane of reality** that the witnesses and survivors of the Colombian **Banana Strike Massacre** (1928) experienced in 100 Years of Solitude. _Include why the real madness is the pretending that the massacre didn't take place._

_____

_____

_____

_____

10) Speculate as to how developing and then adopting a **speculative** approach to understanding history can actually lead to a greater **insight** into understanding events that have happened throughout time.

_____

_____

_____

_____

_____

Invisible Man: Crash Course Literature 308

1) Evaluate **black culture** juxtaposed against the **white culture** as portrayed both inside and outside of the <u>Invisible Man</u> (1952) by Ralph Ellison (1914-1994) in the 1950s.

_____
_____
_____
_____
_____
_____
_____
_____

2) Explain the reasons for the "**Victory at Home! Victory Abroad!**" photography campaign that took place after **World War II** (1939-1945).

_____
_____
_____
_____
_____
_____
_____
_____

3) Analyze how the passage of both ***Brown v. Board of Education (1954)*** as well as the **1964 Civil Rights Act** paved the way for **racial equality** in the United States. *Include why the novel <u>Invisible Man</u> played an important role in the **Civil Rights Movement**.*

_____
_____
_____
_____
_____
_____

4) Evaluate the reasons why the **unnamed black man** and **narrator** of the <u>Invisible Man</u> has problems with both **white culture** and eventually at his job with the **Brotherhood**.

_____
_____
_____
_____
_____
_____
_____

5) Clarify the reasons why the novel <u>Invisible Man</u> still feels relevant today in the **21st century** by taking into account the idea of the **systemic racism**.

_____
_____
_____
_____
_____
_____

6) Analyze the **structure** of the story <u>Invisible Man,</u> and point out why during each **episode** the **narrator** feels more and more **disillusioned** within his **society**.

_____
_____
_____
_____
_____
_____
_____

7) Examine scenes of choice within the novel <u>Invisible Man</u> where the narrator's **invisibility** can be readily apparent by the **people in power** who disregard his **humanity**.

_____
_____
_____
_____
_____
_____
_____

8) Analyze how **Ellison** uses **imagery** inside of the novel <u>Invisible Man</u> to reinforce the idea of the **narrator**'s **invisibility**.

_____
_____
_____
_____
_____
_____

9) Evaluate how race as well as people's **perceptions** of **prejudice** play into the **idea of invisibility** inside the novel <u>Invisible Man</u>.

_____
_____
_____
_____
_____
_____

Sula: Crash Course Literature 309

1) Analyze how the **setting** inside of the fictional **African-American neighborhood** of Medallion, Ohio shapes the novel <u>Sula</u> (1973) by Toni Morrison (1931-Present).

_____
_____
_____
_____

2) Evaluate the essay *Unspeakable Things Unspoken* by Toni Morrison and draw conclusions as to the reasons why Morrison included plants such as **nightshade** and **blackberry** to serve as **metaphors** inside the novel <u>Sula</u>.

_____
_____
_____
_____
_____
_____
_____

3) Compare how Toni Morrison discourages readers against the **binary** thinking of light as good and dark as evil inside of the novel <u>Sula</u>.

_____
_____
_____
_____
_____
_____

4) Investigate how Toni Morrison encourages the reader to reconsider undervalued **identities** and set aside **false binaries** inside of the novel <u>Sula</u>.

_____
_____
_____
_____

5) Draw conclusions as to why **Nel Wright** and **Sula Peace** are friends inside the novel <u>Sula</u>.

_____
_____
_____
_____
_____

6) Cite evidence from the novel <u>Sula</u> that shows how **Hanna** regards **sex**, and then explain how this type of thinking affects **Sula Peace** in the course of her **adult life**.

_____
_____
_____
_____
_____
_____

7) Evaluate the reasons why **Sula Peace** can be seen as both **compelling** and **toxic**.

_____
_____
_____
_____
_____

8) Compare the **internal differences** between **Nel** and **Sula Peace** by analyzing and comparing the great traumatic moments each **character** experienced during **childhood**.

_____
_____
_____
_____
_____
_____
_____

9) Analyze **Sula's desires** for **stability** inside of the **social order** in the novel <u>Sula</u>.

_____
_____
_____
_____
_____
_____
_____

10) Explain the different forms of **freedom** as envisioned by **Sula Peace** inside of <u>Sula</u>.

_____
_____
_____
_____
_____

11) Briefly explain how **Sula** reminds the **reader** that there are both **gains and losses** in any choice.

_____
_____
_____
_____

Crash Course Literature Preview #4

Tip 11) **Tips and Tricks** Notice that the short story "The Yellow Wallpaper," by Charlotte Perkins Gillman is NOT underlined or italicized but instead has quotes surrounding it. This is because it is a short story and when analyzing a short story such as "The Yellow Wallpaper," short stories like it should be cited as such.

*Practice citing short stories, poems, and novels below utilizing the **Tips and Tricks** of all of the Crash Course Literature previews inside of this book.*

Tip 12) **Tips and Tricks** When citing a scene in a play it is best to use Roman numerals to denote which act and scene you are quoting. For example, when citing Act I, scene iii of Macbeth, it is preferable to say Act I scene iii of Macbeth versus Act 1 Scene 3 of Macbeth.

_____
_____
_____
_____
_____
_____
_____
_____
_____
_____
_____
_____
_____
_____
_____
_____
_____
_____
_____
_____
_____
_____
_____
_____
_____
_____
_____
_____
_____
_____
_____
_____
_____
_____
_____
_____

Name_____
Period_____
Date _____

1984 by George Orwell, Part 1: Crash Course Literature 401

1) Analyze how **Winston Smith** not only deals with constant **government surveillance** but is also limited in his thoughts and expressions due to the **totalitarian society** found inside of the novel of <u>1984</u> (1949) by George Orwell (1903-1950).

_____

_____

_____

_____

_____

2) Analyze the **dystopic** ending of <u>1984</u> along with its **dehumanized society** that does NOT have a happy ending but an ending were the bad guys end up winning.

_____

_____

_____

_____

3) Evaluate the mentality of **doublethink** along with the proliferation of contradictory ideas where, "WAR IS PEACE," and "FREEDOM IS SLAVERY," and "IGNORANCE IS STRENGTH."

_____

_____

_____

_____

_____

4) Assess how the life of writer George Orwell aided his rejection of **imperialism** and **colonialism** and helped to shape his **characters** and **plot** inside of his novel <u>1984</u>.

_____

_____

_____

_____

_____

5) Investigate and report on why Orwell rebelled against the "real nature of **capitalist society**," yet still chose to champion the **tenets** of **democratic socialism**.

_____

_____

_____

_____

_____

6) Identify the reasons why George Orwell was NOT in favor of **communism** as it was practiced inside of the socialist state of the **Soviet Union** (1922-1991).

_____

_____

_____

_____

_____

7) Why do YOU think it is difficult for somebody to retain **individual freedoms** within the confines of an **oppressive society**?

_____

_____

_____

_____

8) Evaluate the relationship between **Winston Smith** and **Julia**.

_____

_____

_____

_____

9) Analyze how the political party in charge of the **totalitarian state** of **Oceania** subverts its citizens not only through the tactics of surveillance, arrest, torture, and execution but also by **oppressing language** inside of the novel 1984 by George Orwell.

_____

_____

_____

_____

10) Clarify why the usage of the **Newspeak** vocabulary inside of the novel 1984 by George Orwell is so detrimental to the citizens of **Oceania**.

_____

_____

_____

_____

11) Do YOU think that the **language** YOU use daily helps to give YOU the ability to form and express **complex ideas**? Why or why not? Defend your answer with examples of how language either limits or enhances YOUR daily life.

_____

_____

_____

_____

_____

1984 by George Orwell, Part 2: Crash Course Literature 402

1) Analyze how **structure of language** can be **independent** from **human consciousness** inside the novel <u>1984</u> (1949) by George Orwell (1903-1950).

_____
_____
_____
_____

2) Evaluate what the mutable **doublethink** history that <u>1984</u> **protagonist Winston Smith** of the Records Department of the Ministry of Truth writes about in support of his country of **Oceania**.

_____
_____
_____
_____

3) Construct a hypothesis as to how **Newspeak** narrows the range of thought of the **characters** in the novel <u>1984</u>.

_____
_____
_____
_____

4) How is the political party in power **manipulating memories** in the human brain inside the novel <u>1984,</u> and why do you think they chose to do so?

_____
_____
_____
_____

5) Evaluate to what extent our ability to think is dependent on the **language** we use daily using the following people as a guide:
   a) **Edward Sapir** (1920s) and **Benjamin Whorf** (1950s) -the **Sapir-Whorf Hypothesis**

_____
_____
_____

   b) **Noam Chomsky** (1960s) -**grammarian**

_____
_____
_____

c) Steven Pinker (1990s) -**basic instinct**

_____
_____
_____

6) Explain how **Winston's** instinct to survive drives his conclusion that **humanity** is **inhumane** and by analyzing the relationship between **instinct** and **language** in <u>1984</u>.

_____
_____
_____
_____

7) Explain what happens to **Winston** once he was **psychologically** broken by **Newspeak**.

_____
_____
_____
_____
_____

8) Briefly explain how we know that **free thought** and **free speech** eventually triumph over **physical oppression, psychological oppression**, and **oppressive language**.

_____
_____
_____
_____
_____

9) Do YOU think that YOUR **society** resembles the **society** represented inside of the country of **Oceania** in <u>1984</u>? Why or why not? _Defend your answer using examples._

_____
_____
_____
_____
_____
_____

10) Explain why you are or are NOT in favor of **social media**. _Defend your answer with examples._

_____
_____
_____
_____
_____

The Handmaids Tale (Part 1): Crash Course Literature 403

1) Develop a logical argument as to how a **dystopian society** can remind the reader of the **resilience of humanity** inside of a work of fiction.

_____

_____

_____

_____

_____

_____

2) Explain how Margaret Atwood's (1939-Present) childhood in Quebec, Canada along with her schooling at the University of Toronto helped her to write about **despotism** inside of the fictional government of the **Republic of Giliad** in the The Handmaid's Tale (1985).

_____

_____

_____

_____

_____

_____

3) Analyze the **synopsis** of the **ultra-conservative** and **theocratic** world of The Handmaid's Tale by Margaret Atwood focusing on both the **oppression** and enforced **ignorance** prevalent inside of the **dystopia**.

_____

_____

_____

_____

_____

_____

_____

4) Clarify the multiple meanings of the main character **Offred**'s name in The Handmaid's Tale by Margaret Atwood.

_____

_____

_____

_____

_____

5) Briefly analyze the role of the other **classes of women** in The Handmaid's Tale by Margaret Atwood. i.e. Wives, Econowives, Marthas, and Aunts.

_____

_____

_____

_____

6) Analyze the opening **setting** of the **Rachel and Leah Re-Education Center** inside of The Handmaid's Tale by Margaret Atwood.

_____

_____

_____

_____

7) Evaluate how **desire** has been completely **perverted** in the **Republic of Giliad** inside of The Handmaid's Tale by Margaret Atwood.

_____

_____

_____

_____

_____

8) Connect how Offred's **heroism** allows her to **empathize** with the **commander's wife** even after the she was forced to endure **state-sanctioned rape** in order to become a **surrogate mother**.

_____

_____

_____

_____

9) Evaluate the steep toll that **Offred's mother** paid for being outspoken and critical against the **policies of the government**. *Defend your answer with citations from the novel The Handmaid's Tale by Margaret Atwood.*

_____

_____

_____

_____

10) Clarify why the **genre** of The Handmaid's Tale by Margaret Atwood could be categorized as **speculative fiction**.

_____

_____

_____

The Handmaids Tale (Part 2): Crash Course Literature 404

1) Explain why life for the main character **Offred** has been difficult inside of <u>The Handmaid's Tale</u> (1985) by Margaret Atwood (1939-Present).

_____

_____

_____

_____

_____

_____

2) Analyze whether or not YOU think the novel <u>The Handmaid's Tale</u> by Margaret Atwood is written from a **female point of view**.

_____

_____

_____

_____

3) Evaluate the arguments of **structuralist** theorist Tzvetan Todorov (1939-2017) and the word he coined, narratology, as it pertains to <u>The Handmaid's Tale</u> by Margaret Atwood.

_____

_____

_____

_____

4) Explain how French theorist Hélène Cixous (1937-Present) aided in the advancement of **feminist ideals** as it pertained to the **female human body** and **feminine writing styles**.

_____

_____

_____

_____

5) Clarify the ways in which main character **Offred** is able to express her existence even in the **ultra-conservative** and **oppressive** dystopic world of <u>The Handmaid's Tale</u> by Margaret Atwood. *Cite examples from the novel to defend your answer.*

_____

_____

_____

_____

_____

_____

_____

6) Analyze the reasons for the **storytelling technique** inside of The Handmaid's Tale that focuses on the **human desire** and need to **testify** and connect with someone even when there is no one to connect with.

_____
_____
_____
_____
_____
_____
_____

7) Compare the differences in **perspective** in which the main character **Offred** describes her body from both outside herself and within. *Cite examples from the novel to defend your answer.*

_____
_____
_____
_____
_____
_____
_____
_____

8) Why do YOU think that **Offred** chooses to have sex with **Nick** the gardener?

_____
_____
_____
_____
_____
_____
_____

9) Critique the **classic plot structure** (i.e. Hamlet) against the more **circular plot structure** in The Handmaid's Tale by Margaret Atwood.

_____
_____
_____
_____
_____
_____
_____

10) Critique **Piexoto's lecture** and its reception during the **22nd century** inside of The Handmaid's Tale by Margaret Atwood.

_____
_____
_____
_____
_____

Name_____
Period_____
Date_____

Candide: Crash Course Literature 405

1) Analyze the early life of François-Marie Arouet (1694-1778), aka **Voltaire**, and explain how his genius for comedy put him in the **Bastille** prison in **France** for a year.

_____
_____
_____
_____

2) Analyze **Voltaire**'s belief system which included **Empiricism** and **Religious Tolerance**.
   A) **Empiricism**:

   _____
   _____

   B) **Religious Tolerance**:

   _____
   _____

3) Analyze the early life of **Candide**, where he lived on his uncle's castle (the estate of Baron Trenck), and include his interactions with **Pangloss** and **Cunegonde** as a teenager.

_____
_____
_____
_____

4) Once **Candide** escaped the army, evaluate what he learns from **Pangloss** and **James** about the world.

_____
_____

5) Analyze the phrase, "the best of all possible worlds," uttered over and over again by **Pangloss**, and explain how that phrase relates to the theme of <u>Candide</u> (1759).

_____
_____
_____

6) Compare the term **bildungsroman** to the **satire** rampant in the novel <u>Candide</u> by **Voltaire**.

_____
_____
_____
_____

7) Clarify how <u>Candide</u> can be viewed as an **enlightenment** novel used to inspire thought, and assess why YOU think it was banned in many places.

_____
_____
_____
_____
_____

8) How does **Candide** deal with the **theodicy** and the evil that he encounters inside of the novel of <u>Candide</u>? _Defend your answer using an example._

_____
_____
_____
_____
_____

9) Analyze the argument **Pangloss** gives to **Candide** about how the **Columbian exchange** brought him back the New World disease **syphilis** in the "best of all possible worlds."

_____
_____
_____
_____

10) Evaluate why the novel of <u>Candide</u> embraces the idea that humans love life.

_____
_____
_____
_____
_____

11) Analyze why YOU think **Candide** finds the city of **El Dorado** extremely boring and cannot wait to leave this **Elysium** for his life back in **Europe**.

_____
_____
_____
_____
_____

12) Analyze the reasons why **Candide** eventually rationalizes against **philosophy** and realizes that he should just tend to his own garden and not everybody else's garden.

_____
_____
_____
_____

The Parable of the Sower: Crash Course Literature 406

1) Explain what makes the **dystopic science fiction** novel <u>The Parable of the Sower</u> (1993) by Octavia Butler (1947-2006) not only a **coming-of-age** story but also a story about being **black** and **female** in America.

_____
_____
_____
_____
_____
_____
_____

2) Compare the **thematic** similarities between the <u>Bible</u> (1200 BCE- 100 ACE) and <u>The Parable of the Sower</u> by Octavia Butler.

_____
_____
_____
_____
_____
_____

3) Describe the **home life** of 15-year-old main character **Lauren Oya Olamina** at the beginning of the novel <u>The Parable of the Sower</u> by Octavia Butler.

_____
_____
_____
_____
_____
_____

4) Investigate the **secrets** surrounding the **hyper-empathy** of **Lauren Oya Olamina**.

_____
_____
_____
_____
_____

5) Develop a logical argument as to why **Lauren** creates her own **belief system**, called **Earthseed**, that is centered around locating **God** in chaos, change, and uncertainty.

_____
_____
_____
_____
_____

6) Analyze the two types of **genres** found in <u>The Parable of the Sower</u> by Octavia Butler: **bildungsroman** and **sacred text**.

_____
_____
_____
_____
_____
_____

7) Evaluate how **Lauren** displays her capacity for leadership after her **neighborhood** is overrun by thieves.

_____
_____
_____
_____
_____
_____

8) Clarify how Octavia Butler in her novel <u>The Parable of the Sower</u> draws on elements of **Buddhism**, **Taoism**, **matriarchal religions**, and the **Yoruba religion** in order to create the new religion of **Earthseed**.

_____
_____
_____
_____
_____
_____

9) Analyze the **thematic** current of **change** and show how it is the only **constant** in Lauren's trauma-filled life in <u>The Parable of the Sower</u> by Octavia Butler.

_____
_____
_____
_____
_____
_____

10) In your own words, explain the following **passage**: "God is change,' is an invitation to respond to fear with creativity, productivity, and compassion. [Practitioners must] fully acknowledge and accept suffering and struggle as an inevitable companion to love and happiness," from <u>The Parable of the Sower</u> by Octavia Butler.

_____
_____
_____
_____

The Yellow Wallpaper: Crash Course Literature 407

1) Briefly analyze how the **setting** of a country mansion strengthens the idea of a **dystopia** as found inside the short story "The Yellow Wallpaper," (1892) by **Charlotte Perkins Gillman** (1860-1935).

_____
_____
_____
_____
_____

2) Examine how the **life** of **Charlotte Perkins Gillman** gave her the opportunity to be successful and flourish as a **writer**.

_____
_____
_____
_____
_____

3) Why do YOU think it is important to read "The Yellow Wallpaper," by **Charlotte Perkins Gillman** with the idea that it was created out of her own suffering and **mental illness**?

_____
_____
_____
_____
_____

4) Clarify how **John**, the narrator's husband inside of "The Yellow Wallpaper," belittles his wife **Jane** with his **rest cure** during her battle with **mental illness**.

_____
_____
_____
_____
_____

5) Explain how **sleep deprivation** and **anxiety** can lead to **postpartum depression**.

_____
_____
_____
_____

6) Analyze the reasons why the narrator's keeping of a **journal** about the **yellow wallpaper** is so important to understanding her own **mental illness** inside of "The Yellow Wallpaper." *Cite evidence from the novel to defend your answer.*

_____
_____
_____
_____
_____
_____
_____
_____
_____

7) Investigate the reasons why **patterns** are so important to **Jane** inside of "The Yellow Wallpaper."

_____
_____
_____
_____
_____
_____

8) Draw conclusions as to why **Charlotte Perkins Gillman** would have her narrator **Jane** choose to focus on the **odor** of the **yellow wallpaper**.

_____
_____
_____
_____
_____

9) Why do YOU think **Jane** longs to **free the woman** trapped behind the wallpaper?

_____
_____
_____
_____
_____

10) Analyze the **gender dynamics** captured inside of the short story "The Yellow Wallpaper," by Charlotte Perkins Gillman.

_____
_____
_____
_____
_____
_____

To the Lighthouse: Crash Course Literature 408

1) Examine how the **life** of **Virginia Woolf** (1882-1941), and her **vacations** taken with her family in Cornwall, England may have inspired her to write <u>To the Lighthouse</u> (1927).

_____

_____

_____

_____

_____

2) Analyze the **plot** of <u>To the Lighthouse</u> by of Virginia Woolf and explain why it is considered a **modernist novel**.

_____

_____

_____

_____

_____

_____

3) Clarify the reasons why **modernism** is both **anti-Enlightenment** and **anti-Romantic**.

_____

_____

_____

_____

4) Contrast the differences between the **characters** of **Mr. Ramsay** and **Mrs. Ramsay** inside of the novel <u>To the Lighthouse</u> by Virginia Woolf.

_____

_____

_____

_____

_____

5) Examine the **form** of **modernist novel** <u>To the Lighthouse</u> by Virginia Woolf.

_____

_____

_____

_____

_____

_____

6) Clarify how the both the **tone** and **thinking** of the **vacation house** along with the **changing perspective** (aka the **free indirect discourse**) influences the **style** of the novel To the Lighthouse by Virginia Woolf.

_____
_____
_____
_____
_____
_____

7) Evaluate how Virginia Woolf uses a **stream of consciousness** writing style and blends it with **driving emotion** inside of the novel To the Lighthouse.

_____
_____
_____
_____
_____
_____
_____

8) Analyze how using a **changing of perspective** amplifies the understanding of each of the **characters** inside of the novel To the Lighthouse by Virginia Woolf. _Cite evidence from the novel to back up your claim._

_____
_____
_____
_____
_____
_____

9) Analyze how **time** is suspended during the beef stew **dinner party** and what that does to **memory** and **life** inside of the novel To the Lighthouse by Virginia Woolf. _Cite evidence from the novel to back up your claim._

_____
_____
_____
_____
_____
_____
_____

10) Explain how a **portrait** painted by **Lily** of **Mrs. Ramsay** has the ability to bring her back even after she has died making the moment at the **dinner party** eternal.

_____
_____
_____
_____
_____

Free Will, Witches, Murder, and Macbeth (Part 1): Crash Course Literature 409

1) Critique the **synopsis** and **plot** of the play Macbeth (1606) by William Shakespeare (1564-1616).

_____

_____

_____

_____

_____

2) Connect how the Scottish play Macbeth falls inside the **genre** of both a **tragedy** and **history** interweaving **politics** of his day and in effect updated Holinshed's Chronicles (1577) for modern audiences in **England**.

_____

_____

_____

_____

_____

3) Analyze Act 1, Scene 3 of Macbeth where, after winning battles on their way to **King Duncan's** castle in Forres, **Macbeth** and **Banquo** meet up with **three witches**.

_____

_____

_____

_____

_____

4) Explain how **ambition** and **prophesy** work to shape the **human experience** inside of Macbeth.

_____

_____

_____

_____

5) Evaluate why **King James I** (1566-1625), patron and supporter of William Shakespeare, would defend the **creation** and **distribution** of the play Macbeth at the end of the 16th century.

_____

_____

_____

_____

6) Explain how **King James I** (1566-1625) with the publication of his book on witchcraft <u>Daemonologie</u> (1597) led to more people believing in **supernatural creatures** such as witches, fairies, ghosts, and demons.

_____

_____

_____

_____

_____

_____

_____

7) Critique what YOU think **witch hunt** means. *Defend your answer with examples.*

_____

_____

_____

_____

_____

_____

_____

8) Evaluate the reason why YOU think the play <u>Macbeth</u> has survived throughout the **centuries** and can still be found at **playhouses** in the **21st century**.

_____

_____

_____

_____

_____

_____

_____

9) Analyze the **role** the **witches** play in moving the **plot** inside of the play <u>Macbeth</u>.

_____

_____

_____

_____

_____

_____

_____

10) Analyze the argument surrounding **predestination** during the **Elizabethan Era** (1558-1603) inside of England, and apply concepts to understand why the **topic** was so popular. *Include how this idea of predestination relates to the play <u>Macbeth</u>.*

_____

_____

_____

_____

_____

Gender, Guilt, and Fate- Macbeth (Part 2): Crash Course Literature 410

1) Compare how, in the play <u>Macbeth</u> (1606) by William Shakespeare (1564-1616), the **main character** of **Macbeth**, is both a **hero** and a **villain**.

_____

_____

_____

_____

_____

_____

_____

_____

2) Analyze the reasons that show that **Macbeth's conscience** is troubled due to his murderous actions which cause his **insomnia**. *Cite evidence from the play <u>Macbeth</u> to defend your answer.*

_____

_____

_____

_____

_____

_____

_____

_____

3) Why do YOU think most readers stopped seeing **Macbeth** as a **hero**, at the midpoint of <u>Macbeth</u> after he orders the murder of **Banquo** and his **son**?

_____

_____

_____

_____

_____

4) Analyze the meaning of the statement uttered by the **witches** in **Macbeth**, "Something wicked this way comes."

_____

_____

_____

_____

_____

_____

5) Explain how **Lady Macbeth** talks **Macbeth** into killing **King Duncan**.

_____

_____

_____

_____

_____

6) Draw conclusions as to why **Lady Macbeth** would become so disturbed by her deed so as to mime washing her hands over and over while **sleepwalking** through the **Castle Inverness**.

_____

_____

_____

_____

_____

_____

7) Evaluate how the play <u>Macbeth</u> treats **masculinity** and **femininity**.

_____

_____

_____

_____

_____

8) Clarify how **Lady Macbeth** attacks **Macbeth**'s **masculinity** for his initial refusal to kill **Duncan**, and how her attack on his **masculinity** may have driven him to murder.

_____

_____

_____

_____

_____

9) Analyze **Act IV Scene iii** of <u>Macbeth</u> where **Macbeth's masculinity** is questioned by the characters **Malcolm** and **Macduff**.

_____

_____

_____

_____

_____

10) Do YOU think that **Macbeth**'s death is **predestined** to happen or that his death comes about due to the choices that he made throughout the play <u>Macbeth</u>?

_____

_____

_____

Pride and Prejudice Part 1: Crash Course English Literature 411

1) Analyze the reasons why YOU think the **themes** and **characters** inside the **social satire** novel <u>Pride and Prejudice</u> (1813) by Jane Austin (1775-1817) have remained relevant throughout the centuries.

_____
_____
_____
_____

2) Compare the **similarities** inside of **Jane Austin**'s life with her novel <u>Pride and Prejudice</u>.

_____
_____
_____
_____

3) Evaluate the social, political, and economic **context** of **19th century England**, and analyze how that may have affected the novel <u>Pride and Prejudice</u> by Jane Austin.

_____
_____
_____
_____
_____

4) Evaluate the reasons why **women** didn't have many **rights** at the beginning of the **19th century** of which can be seen in the novel <u>Pride and Prejudice</u> by Jane Austin.

_____
_____
_____
_____
_____

5) Analyze how both **periods** of the **American Revolution** (1765-1783) and the **French Revolution** (1789-1799) unsettled the established **social** and **political order** and lead to **natural rights** and **equality** for all citizens.

_____
_____
_____
_____
_____
_____

6) Evaluate why YOU think **Jane Austin** would not describe **events** in detail inside her novel <u>Pride and Prejudice</u>.

_____
_____
_____
_____
_____
_____
_____

7) Show how <u>Pride and Prejudice</u> by Jane Austin is a novel that is **suspicious** of **romantic love**. _Cite an example from the novel to defend your answer._

_____
_____
_____
_____
_____
_____
_____
_____

8) Briefly explain how <u>Pride and Prejudice</u> explores how **social interaction** and **social experience** forms the basis for the bonds of love between its various **characters**.

_____
_____
_____
_____
_____
_____

9) Analyze how Jane Austin invents the **style** of **free indirect discourse** and then runs with it inside of her novel <u>Pride and Prejudice</u>.

_____
_____
_____
_____
_____
_____
_____

10) Defend how Jane Austin allows the reader to **empathize** with and become **Elizabeth** by using a unique **narrative approach** inside of the novel <u>Pride and Prejudice</u>.

_____
_____
_____
_____
_____

Liberals, Conservatives, and Pride and Prejudice Part 2: Crash Course English Literature 412

1) Evaluate why **epistemology**, aka the study of knowledge, is a real problem for the **characters** inside of the **plot** of Pride and Prejudice (1813) by Jane Austin.

_____

_____

_____

_____

_____

2) Analyze why characters inside of Pride and Prejudice (1813) which takes place in Regency, **England** have to rely on **gossip, subtle inquiries**, and what they can see with their own eyes in order to glean information about each other.

_____

_____

_____

_____

_____

_____

3) Briefly explain the meaning of the **title** of the book Pride and Prejudice (1813) by Jane Austin and show how that relates to the **characters** of **Elizabeth Bennet** and **Mr. Fitzwilliam Darcy**.

_____

_____

_____

4) Evaluate what **Elizabeth** acknowledges about her own **prejudices** surrounding **Darcy** and **Wickham**. *Defend your answer with a **quote** from the novel Pride and Prejudice.*

_____

_____

_____

_____

_____

5) Analyze what the author **Jane Austin** is reminding the reader when **Elizabeth** asks the question, "What could be the meaning of it?" in Pride and Prejudice.

_____

_____

_____

_____

6) Choose a few **characters** from <u>Pride and Prejudice</u> and clarify how the amount of money they have plays a role in **shaping** their future.

_____

_____

_____

_____

_____

_____

_____

7) Evaluate how the growing **industrialization** of **England** in the early **19th century** played a role in the **material wealth** of the **characters** inside of <u>Pride and Prejudice</u>.

_____

_____

_____

_____

_____

_____

_____

8) Explain how and why **Elizabeth** falls in love with **Darcy**. *Include how some could see this as an example of* **materialism**.

_____

_____

_____

_____

_____

_____

9) Do YOU think <u>Pride and Prejudice</u> (1813) by Jane Austin is **liberal** or **conservative** in its outlook? *Defend your answer.*

_____

_____

_____

_____

_____

_____

10) Draw conclusions as to how **Elizabeth's claim** of **full personhood** in the novel <u>Pride and Prejudice</u> is actually **revolutionary** in thought and echoes sentiments of <u>The Declaration of Independence</u> (1776).

_____

_____

_____

_____

_____

Tip 13) **Tips and Tricks** Many times it is better to provide a "middle of the sentence," quote structure analysis versus a lengthy citation or quote (over one sentence). Find your words, quote them simply, then cite the author who said it prior to your analysis on those words.

Practice **citing** here or use any extra sentence lines located on the back of this book

_____
_____
_____
_____
_____
_____
_____
_____
_____
_____
_____
_____
_____
_____
_____
_____

Tip 14) **Tips and Tricks** When citing a book such as <u>100 Years of Solitude</u> it is customary to underline the name of the book if you are writing it down on paper as in this book. BUT if you are typing it on a computer, it is customary to put the book name *100 Years of Solitude* in italics as is done in the Table of Contents of this book. For the sake of personal writing consistency, this workbook will be underlining the names of books in order to facilitate writing learning style as you practice in this workbook.

***Practice **writing** and **underlining** book titles here* **

_____
_____
_____
_____
_____
_____
_____
_____
_____
_____
_____
_____
_____
_____

Glossary

Absurdity = The state of being ridiculous.

Acronym = An abbreviation using the first letters of a word.

Aka = Also known as.

Allegiance = To pledge or be loyal towards someone or something.

Ambition = Having a strong desire to do or to achieve something.

American Revolution = A colonial revolt against England which occurred between 1765-1783 and established the United States of America.

Antagonist = An adversary.

Anti-bildungsroman = A story where the main character never attains maturity and the character is disillusioned by the end of the novel.

Apathetic = Showing no interest or enthusiasm towards something or someone.

Argument = A reason or set of reasons given to persuade others that an action or idea is right or wrong.

Attributes = A quality or feature of something or someone.

Autobiography = A book written about yourself.

Background = The circumstances or situation around a particular time or event.

Banana republic = A politically unstable country with its economy dependent on a few exported items.

Bildungsroman = A story about the coming of age of its character from youth to an adult.

Binary = Relating to or involving two things.

Boundary = A line that marks the limits of an area.

Blasé = Indifferent or not impressed.

Brown v. Board of Education (1954) = A landmark Supreme Court ruling that overturned *Plessy v. Ferguson* (1896) and legally granted equality to all people regardless of race or color.

Buddhism = A religion that seeks to understand the nature of suffering and the elimination of that suffering.

Capitalist society = A society that follows the economic system of capitalism.

Capitalism = An economic system where private enterprise and businesses are controlled by owners for profit rather than controlled and owned by the state.

Character = A person in a novel or play.

Character arc = The transformation of a character over the course of a story.

Christianity = A religion based upon the teachings of Jesus of Nazareth.

Circular plot structure = A non-linear plot structure that advances more or less chronologically with the protagonist returning to the situation similar to one at the beginning of the story.

Cite = To quote.

Civilization = The most advanced stage of human social and cultural development.

Civil duty = The principle that citizens owe some allegiance to their government.

Classic plot structure = Structure of a story that follows the rise of the hero (protagonist) followed by a conflict, then rising action with more conflict, that leads to the climax of that story, then followed by a resolution.

Climax = The apex or the most intense and important point in a novel or play.

Colombian Exchange = The widespread transfer of plants, animals, diseases, and human cultures between the Old World (Europe and West Africa) and the New World (the Americas).

Colonialism = A government that acquires control over another region and occupies it with settlers and many times exploits the region economically.

Colloquial style = Informal language spoken as a distinct form of literary English.

Commentary = An expression of opinions about a situation.

Commerce = The business of buying and selling on a large scale.

Communal = Something that belongs to everyone and is shared between all.

Communism = An economic system where business is owned by the state rather than privately controlled by owners for profit.

Canon = A general rule from which a literary work is judged.

Century = A period of 100 years.

Certainty = Something that is 100% true or believed to be 100% true.

Claim = A demand or request for something one believes belongs to them.

Class = A system found in an ordered society where people are divided into social and economic status.

Conscience = An inner feeling or voice that works as a guide on how one should behave.

Conservative = A person who follows traditional values and is cautious about change.

Constant = Something that remains the same.

Context = The circumstances that form the setting of an event.

Controversial = Something that is likely to be disagreed upon.

Corpse = A dead person.

Counterargument = An argument that is in opposition to a theory developed in another argument.

Critic = A person who professionally judges the merit of something i.e. art, literature, plays, movies, etc.

Democratic socialism = A type of government where the poor working class is in charge of both the economy and the government.

Depiction = A representation in words or images of someone or something.

Desire = Wanting something.

Dialogue = A conversation between two or more people.

Double standard = A rule that is applied to one group and not another.

Doublethink = The practice of accepting two contradictory and opposing viewpoints as mutually correct. e.g. Feeling strongly and following a course of life that champions the tenets held between both the Republican Party and Democrat Party in the United States.

Dramatic shift = Striking and effective narration that has a sudden and emotional impact.

Dysfunctional = Not being able to function or act properly.

Dystopia = An imagined state of society where there is great suffering. It is the exact opposite of a utopia.

e.g. = Latin for, "exempla gratia." In English it means, "for example."

etc. = Acronym used at the end of a sentence to indicate that similar items are included.

El Dorado = The term used by the Spanish Empire to describe a fictional city completely made of gold.

Enlightenment = An intellectual movement that began in Europe that emphasized the philosophy of reason and individualism rather than tradition.

Empathize =To understand and share the feelings of another.

Empiricism = A sensory-based philosophy stimulated by the rise of experimental science.

Epistemology = the study of knowledge with the understanding that opinion is different from fact.

Exploitative = Treating others unfairly in order to glean some type of benefit.

Exposition = An explanation of an idea or theory.

i.e. = First letters of, "in essence." It is an abbreviation for, "in other words."

False binaries = a type of closed-minded black and white thinking where there is no room for a middle ground.

Familial = Relating to things in a family.

Fate = Destined to happen or turn out in a particular way."

Fatal flaw = A weakness a hero has of which constantly makes them unhappy and opens them up for conflicts throughout the course of their lifetime.

Free indirect discourse = A type of third-person narration that uses phrases to slip in and out of the consciousness of a character.

Femininity = Character traits normally associated with women.

Feminist = A person who champions the rights of females.

Fiction = Literature that describes imaginary events and people.

Fictionalized = To give a fictional account of.

Flashback = A memory of a past event remembered in the present.

Form = The shape and structure of something or someone.

Free will = The ability to act how you want or do whatever you want to do and having the ability to choose between different possible courses at your own discretion.

French Revolution = A violent decade-long revolution that began in 1789 and culminated with the overthrow of Louis XVI (1754-1793), the rise of the 3rd estate, and the establishing of Napoleon (1769-1821) as Emperor of the French.

Gender = The sex of a person.

Generation = All the people born or living around the same time and normally inside of a thirty-year time frame.

Genre = A category in literature that is characterized by similarities in style, form, or subject matter.

Gossip = Rumor spread about the private affairs of others.

Government surveillance = The continuous observation by a government upon its people by a number of different means.

Grammar = The bits and pieces, i.e. syntax and morphology, that make up the whole system and structure of a language.

Grammarian = A person who studies the tenets of grammar.

Hallmark = To designate for distinction or excellence.

Harbinger = A person, thing, or event that announces the coming of something or approach of another.

Harlem Renaissance = A period of time of intellectual, artistic, and social growth centered in Harlem, New York during the 1920s.

Havoc = The act of causing chaos.

Heroic = A brave action undertaken by a hero.

Historical context = Important events that occur during a specific time that define that specific era.

Historical significance = The reasons why something is so important based upon when it happened in history.

Homonym = Two words having the same spelling but different meanings.

Humanity = The collective that makes up the human race.

Hyper-empathy = The act of being extremely sensitive to emotions and energies of people, animals, and elements in the environment.

Iambic pentameter = A line of verse with five metrical feet, each consisting of one short (or unstressed) syllable followed by on long (or stressed) syllable.

Idealization = Regarding something or someone as better than the actual reality.

Ideals = A set of standards to attain perfection.

Identity = Something that someone is most like or relates to shapes who they perceive themselves as.

Indecisiveness = Not being able to make a decision.

Ideological = Following a system of ideas or ideals.

Idiosyncrasy = Nuances or the particular mode of behavior of someone or something.

Ignorance = Lack of knowledge on a particular subject. Many times this can be an individual or societal choice made to not see or attempt not to see or understand the validity of a moral way of thinking due to extreme pigheadedness or at times plain apathy.

Imperialism = Extending a country's power and influence through diplomatic channels or through the military at times by force.

Imagery = The author's use of vivid and descriptive language to add depth to a work.

Incarceration = Imprisoned.

Indecisiveness = Not able to make a decision.

Individual freedoms = The absence of people being able to think for themselves.

Industrialization = The development of industry on a wide scale.

Inhumane = Cruel. A wicked action.

Inquiry = To ask for information.

Insight = The power to see into a situation.

Instinct = an embedded desire to do something even though it has not been formally or informally taught.

Irony = A way of using language or a situation that normally means the opposite of the way it is actually said or presented. A good example is a store window that has a sign indicating the store is going out of business, yet it is placed next to another sign that says, "now hiring."

Language = Words used by characters to communicate between each other or to explain a story.

Liberal = A person who is open to new opinions and willing to discard traditional values.

Literary effect = Techniques writers use to create a specific effect inside of their writing.

Literary genre = A style of writing.

Logic = Reasoning that follows strict principals of truth that can be verified.

Magical Realism = Fantastic or mystical elements woven into realistic fiction.

Manipulate = the ability to make somebody or a group of people do or think something else by shaping their reality in order to achieve a desired outcome.

Masculinity = Character traits normally associated with men.

Materialism = The idea that material possessions and physical comfort are held on a pedestal.

Metaphor = A figure of speech in which a word or a phrase is applied to an object or action. Good examples would be, "my teacher is a dragon," or "he is a night owl."

Millennia = Plural for millennium. Thousands of years.

Millennium = A thousand years.

Misogynistic = A quality possessed by somebody that make take the form of overt actions to show that that person does not like women.

Modernism = A style or movement in art that aims to break with the traditional or classical forms.

Morality = Principals that shed light upon the differences between what is right and what is wrong.

Mortality = The state of being subject to death.

Myth = A traditional story which explains some natural or social phenomenon.

Mythology = The study of myths woven into both oral and written stories which at many times include fantastic characters or creatures or gods and is passed down through the generations.

Multigenerational = Spanning several generations.

Natural resources = Materials found in nature such as minerals, forests, water, and land that can be used for monetary gain.

Narcissism = An egotistic admiration of oneself.

Narrative = A story.

Narrator = The person in charge of clarifying the story in a play or novel.

Neocolonialism = A country that makes use of economic, cultural, and political means in order to control another country.

Non-confrontational = Not wanting to confront something and rather deal with diplomatically.

Non-linear = Circuitous and jumping around rather than following a straight time line.

Objective = A way of looking at things where a person's point of view is not influenced by personal feelings or opinions.

Objectification = Degrading someone to a wanton object.

Oppression = A prolonged and cruel treatment of a person or people.

Oppressive = To inflict unnecessary hardship upon a particular person or group of people.

Overconfidence = Having an extraordinary amount of confidence in something or oneself.

Outlawing = To make illegal.

Passage = A section of a book or play.

Passive = Submissive. Not confrontational so much so as to allow or accept what happens to yourself or others without going against.

Perception = One's senses that have the ability to hear, see, or become aware of something.

Period = A length of time.

Perspective = The way a person or character sees the world.

Perverted = Something that has been altered or corrupted from its initial state.

Phenomena = An observable event such as gravity or tidal forces.

Philosophy = The study of the fundamental qualities of existence.

Plane of reality = A multi-dimensional way of looking at the universe where the plane of reality consists of the physical plane.

Play = A theatrical performance.

Plot = The main elements inside of a play, story, or novel.

Political order = The idea that the ruling governmental body has a set of rules to be followed by its constituents in order to maintain the status quo.

Portrait = A picture of something or somebody.

Psychological = Arising in the mind and related to the mental and emotional state of a person.

Psychological realism = A literary method in which the author focuses their characters on interior motives and mental narratives rather than by just telling a story.

Predestination = The idea that all events are willed by God and that everything is already pre-planned.

Prejudice = Preconceived opinion that is not based upon reason or experience.

Protagonist = The hero of a novel or play.

Pseudonyms = Another name used by writers in place of their own name that at many times is fictitious i.e. not real, and has been created for a variety of reasons.

Public defender = Somebody who defends a person - normally a lawyer - in a court of law

Quote = To repeat passage from a book or a statement by a person.

Race = Biologically similar traits shared between a number of people.

Reality = The state of things that actually exist.

Reanimate = To make alive again after initially dead.

Religious Tolerance = People allowing other people to think and practice religion in the way that every person wishes to practice religion including beliefs in different ideologies, philosophies, and deities.

Repetition = The act of repeating something that has already been said or written.

Revisionism = The practice of revising one's principles or attitude from a previously held point of view.

Revolutionary = A dramatic change caused by the engagement in a revolution. A person involved in social and political change.

Rhyming schemes = A pattern of rhymes normally at the end of each line in a poem or a song.

Rights = Normal rules dictated by society surrounding the concept of freedom.

Role = An actor's part in a play.

Satire = The use of humor, irony, and exaggeration to amplify the ridiculousness of person's behavior.

Scandalous = Something that causes or could cause general outrage by the public.

Science fiction = Fiction written about events happening in the future that is imagined by the author.

Setting = The place or surroundings where an event takes place.

Slant rhyme = An imperfect rhyme where instead of a perfect rhyme in a poem at the end of a line. E.g. if the third and fourth line in a perfect rhyme ended "take," and "snake" respectively than the slant rhyme would be written, "tape" and "snake."

Social experience = Interactions between people that are important in establishing social connections.

Social order = The idea that various components of a society such as its social structures and social institutions follow a set of norms, beliefs, and values meant to maintain the status quo.

Social satire = A satirical critique that makes fun of preconceived notions of how somebody should act in a social situation.

Society = The people living in a community in a certain area.

Soviet Union = The Union of Soviet Socialist Republics that existed after the violent overthrow of Tsar Nicholas II (1868-1918) in the early 20th century during World War I by the proletariat working class in Russia until the early 1990s.

Speculative = A form of questioning that asks why something is the way it is.

Stability = An unchanging quality of a situation favored by many ordered societies.

Statement = Something that somebody says.

Status quo = Normality. The existing state of affairs of things meant to be continued as it were.

Story telling technique = The way in which an author tells a story.

Structuralism = A methodology which implies that elements of human culture are understood in a way that relates to the much larger system or structure.

Structuralist = a person that adheres to the philosophy of structuralism.

Structure = A story is made up of a series of events of which the layout of these events make up that story's structure.

Style = The reference to form, appeal, or character.

Subjective = A way of looking at things where a person's point of view is influenced by their personal feelings or opinions.

Subversive = Words or actions going against what is considered normal. By doing so, these words or actions may have a harmful effect upon the status quo of what is moral in a society.

Supernatural creatures = Animals or unnatural hybrids of humans which originate from non-earthly dimensions.

Symbology = The use of symbols to represent something else in a novel or play.

Synopsis = An outline of a book or a play.

Syphilis = A new world disease that spread to Europe during the Columbian exchange.

Systemic racism = Racism that is upheld by the system of government that is part of a society.

Taoism = A religion that seeks to live in peace and harmony with nature.

Tenet = A principal or belief.

Testify = To give evidence as a witness in court.

Thematic example = An example that addresses the main topic of a story and pinpoints an author's viewpoint. E.g. Hamlet is a tragic story about a character who must take revenge on another character in the play.

Theme = An idea that keeps recurring inside of a story.

Theodicy = The understanding that good exists as providence by also understanding about why God permits the existence of evil.

Theological = Relating to religion or the study of religion.

Theology = The study of the nature of God.

Titan = A race of Greek deities.

Title = Name of a book.

Tone = The general feeling surrounding a place, a piece of writing, or a situation.

Topic = The main idea inside of a sentence or about what is being said.

Totalitarian government = A government with complete control over its citizens.

Tragedy = A play dealing with unfortunate events along with a unhappy ending.

Utopia = An imagined state of society where everything is perfect.

Vernacular speech = The way in which somebody in a certain region or place speaks.

Victorian Era (1837-1901) = A period of time which followed the reign of England's Queen Victoria.

Vision = The idea or mental image of something.

Voice = Characteristic speech and thought patterns of the narrator in a novel.

Witch = A woman that has magical powers.

World War I = A major war fought all over the world in the early 20th century that saw a network of entangling alliances become involved in wars all around the world with the Allied Powers eventually defeating the Central Powers.

World War II = A major series of wars fought all over the world in the mid-20th century characterized by a major conflict of ideologies between the leading countries of Nazi Germany, Imperialist Japan, and Fascist Italy lining up against the United States, Soviet Union, and Great Britain of which the latter proved victorious setting up a new world order.

Yoruba (religion) = A set of beliefs that involves ritual practices of singing, dancing, divination, spirit possession, and ritual healing in order to worship previous ancestors.

13th Amendment = Abolished slavery in the United States.

14th Amendment = Granted citizenship to all persons born in the United States.

15th Amendment = Granted African American men the right to vote in the United States.

Notes

Notes

Notes

Notes

Notes

Notes

Notes

Notes

Notes

Notes

Notes

Notes

Awesome Links

Visit and follow my public Facebook page at rogermorante@rogermorante13 Comments and "likes" welcome!! ☺

Specials discounts on bulk orders and class sets over 30 also available. Please contact holden713@gmail.com with your query to make arrangements for your discounted order.

Other books of interest by Roger Morante and available for purchase on Amazon include:

Crash Course US History: A Study Guide of Worksheets for US History

Crash Course World History: A Study Guide of Worksheets for World History

Crash Course Government and Politics: A Study Guide of Worksheets for Government and Politics

Crash Course Economics: A Study Guide of Worksheets for Economics

Crash Course Psychology: A Study Guide of Worksheets for Psychology (Release Date November 2019)

Made in the USA
Monee, IL
06 May 2021